"America's leading source of self-help information." ★★★★
—YAHOO!

C0-CFB-753

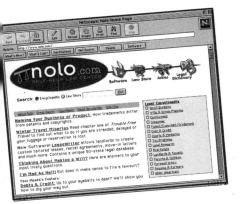

LEGAL INFORMATION ONLINE ANYTIME

24 hours a day

www.nolo.com

AT THE NOLO.COM SELF-HELP LAW CENTER, YOU'LL FIND

- Nolo's comprehensive Legal Encyclopedia filled with plain-English information on a variety of legal topics
- Nolo's Law Dictionary—legal terms <u>without</u> the legalese
- Auntie Nolo—if you've got questions, Auntie's got answers
- The Law Store—over 250 self-help legal products including: Downloadable Software, Books, Form Kits and eGuides
- Legal and product updates
- Frequently Asked Questions
- NoloBriefs, our free monthly email newsletter
- Legal Research Center, for access to state and federal statutes
- Our ever-popular lawyer jokes

Quality LAW BOOKS & SOFTWARE FOR EVERYONE

Nolo's user-friendly products are consistently first-rate. Here's why:

- A dozen in-house legal editors, working with highly skilled authors, ensure that our products are accurate, up-to-date and easy to use
- We continually update every book and software program to keep up with changes in the law
- Our commitment to a more democratic legal system informs all of our work
- We appreciate & listen to your feedback. Please fill out and return the card at the back of this book.

OUR "NO-HASSLE" GUARANTEE

Return anything you buy directly from Nolo for any reason and we'll cheerfully re-fund your purchase price. No ifs, ands or buts.

AN IMPORTANT MESSAGE TO OUR READERS

This product provides information and general advice about the law. But laws and procedures change frequently, and they can be interpreted differently by different people. For specific advice geared to your specific situation, consult an expert. No book, software or other published material is a substitute for personalized advice from a knowledgeable lawyer licensed to practice law in your state.

Domain Names

HOW TO CHOOSE AND PROTECT A GREAT NAME FOR YOUR WEBSITE

BY ATTORNEYS STEVE ELIAS
AND PATRICIA GIMA

nolo

Codman Sq. Branch Library
690 Washington Street
Dorchester, MA 02124
DEC   2000

KEEPING UP-TO-DATE

To keep its books up-to-date, Nolo issues new printings and new editions periodically. New printings reflect minor legal changes and technical corrections. New editions contain major legal changes, major text additions or major reorganizations. To find out if a later printing or edition of any Nolo book is available, call Nolo at 510-549-1976 or check our website at www.nolo.com.

To stay current, follow the "Update" service at our website at www.nolo.com. In another effort to help you use Nolo's latest materials, we offer a 35% discount off the purchase of the new edition of your Nolo book when you turn in the cover of an earlier edition. (See the "Special Upgrade Offer" in the back of the book.) This book was last revised in March 2000.

FIRST EDITION	**March 2000**
EDITOR	Mary Randolph
PROOFREADER	Robert Wells
INDEXER	Ellen Davenport
COVER	Toni Ihara
PRINTING	Bertlesmann Industry Services

CD BR
TK5105
.875
.I57
E43
2000

Elias, Stephen.
    Domain names : how to choose and protect a great name for your website / by Stephen Elias and Patricia Gima.
       p.   cm.
    ISBN 0-87337-569-6
    1. Internet domain names. I. Gima, Patricia. II. Title.
    TK5105.875.I57 E43 2000
    004.67'8--dc   99-052900
                                                                   CIP

Copyright © 2000 by Stephen Elias and Patricia Gima. All Rights Reserved. Printed in the U.S.A.

No part of this publication may be reproduced, stored in a retrieval system, or transmitted in any form or by any means, electronic, mechanical, photocopying, recording or otherwise without prior written permission.

Quantity sales: For information on bulk purchases or corporate premium sales, please contact the Special Sales department. For academic sales or textbook adoptions, ask for Academic Sales, 800-955-4775, Nolo.com, 950 Parker St., Berkeley, CA 94710.

ACKNOWLEDGMENTS

Thanks to Patti Gima, my wonderful co-author, and to Mary Randolph for her marvelous editing and ever-cheerful support for this book. Thanks also to the many wonderful folks at Nolo who keep the Nolo flame burning bright and bring our goods to market.

DEDICATIONS

To Rubin Santiago Elias, a good friend, great son and true child of the Internet.

—Steve Elias

ACKNOWLEDGMENTS

Many thanks to my husband, Joe, and my son, Jordan, for their unwavering support. Thank you, Mary Randolph, for your precision editing. Thanks, Steve Elias, for being a great co-author. Thanks, too, to Terri Hearsh for the swift and wonderful book layout.

DEDICATION

I'd like to dedicate this book (or my portion of it ;-)) to Jordan and Joe. Two constant sources of creativity.

Patricia Gima

Contents

CHAPTER 7

HOW TO TELL WHETHER CUSTOMER CONFUSION IS LIKELY

CHAPTER 8

HOW TO REGISTER YOUR DOMAIN NAME AS A TRADEMARK

CHAPTER 9

HELP BEYOND THIS BOOK

APPENDIX

INDEX

Icons Used in this Book

 Caution: A potential problem.

 See an Expert: An instance when you may need the advice of an attorney or other expert.

 Tip: A bit of advice that may help you with a particular issue.

 Resources: Books, websites or other resources that may be of use.

 Fast Track: Lets you know that you may be able to skip some material.

KEEPING UP TO DATE

The world of domain names is changing as fast as the Internet itself, but books are difficult to keep up-to-date between editions. We'll post significant new developments in the Updates section of www.nolo.com. Checking there should keep you current.

■

The Legal Side of Domain Names

To do business on the Web, you'll need at least one domain name— the yada-yada-dot-com that has become so familiar in commercials and print advertising. Your domain name may be the name you already use for a business, with a dot-com added, or a new name that you think will do a good job of getting people to your website. If you follow the lead of many businesses, you'll use multiple domain names to help the widest possible number of potential customers find your site among the many thousands out there.

Choosing a name, or more than one, for your website is no trivial matter—your decisions can make or break your business. This explains why some domain names have been auctioned off for huge amounts of money. The current record-holder is business.com, which went for an astounding $7.5 million. The winning bidder apparently believes the name has enough customer-drawing power to make it worthwhile. Fortunately for small e-commerce start-ups with limited budgets, most businesses make up their domain names or use names that they are already using as trademarks, and don't pay anyone a penny for the privilege.

DOMAIN NAME ANATOMY

Domain names consist of two main parts: the top-level domain name, or TLD, and the second-level domain name, or SLD. The SLD comes first. For example, in nolo.com, nolo is the SLD.

The TLD comes at the end of the domain name, after the ubiquitous dot. TLDs are organized, for U.S. participants, into five categories:

- .com, for commercial groups
- .edu, for educational institutions
- .gov, for governmental entities
- .org, for nonprofit organizations, and
- .net, for interactive discussion groups.

Other countries have their own TLDs—for example, .fr for France, .gr for Greece, .to for Tonga.

It's the SLD that makes your domain name unique. Almost all U.S. businesses choose to operate under the .com domain. There are plans to introduce a number of new TLDs, such as .inc and .stor, but it hasn't happened yet. And even when it does, most businesses are still going to want to be "dotcoms."

A. Thinking About the Law

You may have thought a lot about the marketing aspects of your domain name—how the name can attract visitors, communicate what you do, stick in customers' minds and inspire confidence in your business. All those factors definitely deserve attention, but there's another set of concerns that is at least as important: how trademark law affects your choice and use of a name.

If your domain name is the same as or similar to a trademark already being used by a competing or related business, that business might force you to stop using it somewhere down the road. And if you have built up considerable goodwill under the domain name when a trademark conflict flares up, this could amount to a business catastrophe. You can avoid this potential disaster by picking a domain name that is free and clear from legal conflicts.

IF SOMEONE CHALLENGES YOUR DOMAIN NAME

This book is not designed to help you if your existing domain name comes under legal attack—for instance, if another business demands that you surrender your domain name. If that happens, we recommend *Trademark: Legal Care for Your Product and Service Name,* by Stephen Elias and Kate McGrath (Nolo), or to Nolo's downloadable eGuide, *Trademark Disputes: Who Wins, Who Loses & Why.* You may also need to consult a lawyer.

Some names are wonderful from a commercial perspective but close enough to existing names to cause a legal tiff, such as the dispute between etoys.com, a large toy dealer, and etoy.com, a small website of some English artists. Still other names may be unique as domain names but identical or confusingly similar to names used by brick-and-mortar-companies—a fact which easily can give rise to a trademark infringement lawsuit.

Fortunately, you can select a domain name that will be both commercially appropriate for your business and free from legal challenges by other businesses. Your best strategy may be to leverage an existing business name, with strong customer recognition, by using it (or part of it) as your domain name. But if you're just starting out, you may want to invent something catchy and different.

B. Protecting the Name You Choose

To be sure that your name really is different—not identical to or similar enough to someone else's trademarked name—you need to search for available domain names and register your domain name with a domain name registry service. The next step is to file an application with the U.S. Patent and Trademark Office to register your domain name as a trademark.

STEPS IN CHOOSING AND RESERVING A DOMAIN NAME

☐ If you've picked out a domain name, reserve it so it won't get snapped up by another business. (Chapter 2)

☐ If you haven't yet chosen a domain name, select one that will get people to your website and also qualify for protection as a trademark. (Chapters 3 and 4)

☐ If your preferred name is taken, consider alternate names and your legal options. (Chapter 5)

☐ Use the Internet to search for existing trademarks that legally conflict with your name. (Chapters 6 and 7)

☐ If your name conflicts with an existing trademark, choose another name (Chapter 4) or, if you are already using the name as a mark, assert your rights as a trademark owner. (Chapter 5)

☐ For maximum protection for your name, apply for federal trademark registration. (Chapter 8)

■

How to Reserve a Domain Name

If you've already chosen a domain name, your first step should be to register it with a domain name registration service. This will give you the exclusive right to use that domain name.

You may want to register a name—or more than one—even if you haven't yet searched for possible trademark conflicts (see Chapter 6) or made a final decision about your domain name. Websites are going up in great numbers, and if you wait, you may lose the name you want. You do risk wasting the amount of the reservation or registration fee if you later decide to use a different name. But that risk may be worth it if you do ultimately decide to use your first choice and you've managed to prevent someone else from grabbing it first.

Example: *Geoff wants to use the domain name doctortrademark.com for his website, which offers legal advice on trademarks. He checks the availability of that name and learns that it has been taken. Geoff then checks drtrademark.com and finds that it's available. Although Geoff knows (because he has read Chapter 7) that using such a similar domain name might infringe the doctortrademark.com trademark, he decides to go ahead and reserve the name until he can do some more investigation regarding the other "Doctor Trademark" website.*

If the exact domain name you want has been taken by someone else, you will not be able to register it unless you have already been using the name as a trademark and are willing to take the steps described in Chapter 5 to assert your legal rights as a trademark owner.

Don't be a cybersquatter. It is against federal law to register someone else's personal or business name as your domain name, if you're doing it because you want to sell the name back to its owner for a profit.

If you are choosing a domain name for the purpose of using it on a website that will be doing legitimate commerce, you have nothing to worry about. However, if you are buying up domain names so you can sell them later, you should definitely get some advice from a lawyer about the legality of your activity. The federal Anti-Cybersquatting Consumer Protection Act, the law that prohibits cybersquatting, is discussed in detail in Chapter 5.

A. Where to Register

A number of new domain name registration agencies are getting ready to open their electronic doors. (See "New Domain Name Registries," below.) For now, however, we recommend that you use Network Solutions, Inc., to check the availability of and register your name. NSI is the leading domain name registrar in the world, with over five million registrations to date and, until mid-1999, was the only U.S. registry. We base our recommendation primarily on NSI's successful track record; the newer registries, while competitive in terms of price, lack NSI's experience.

NEW DOMAIN NAME REGISTRIES

The international group that is now in charge of Internet domain name policy (ICANN, short for International Corporation for Assigned Names and Numbers) is in the process of chartering a number of additional domain name registering agencies. All of these agencies use a shared, central registry, maintained by NSI, so that there will be no duplications. The main stated purpose of having a number of registering agencies is to foster competition. While NSI is still the main game in town, more choices may mean lower registration fees. A list of approved domain name registries is available at www.internic.net/alpha.html.

After checking the availability of your name with NSI, you can either register it or reserve it with a credit card. If you want to register the name, you must be prepared to give NSI information about your Internet Service Provider (ISP) and about who will be physically maintaining (hosting) your website. If you don't have immediate plans to attach your domain name to a website, or haven't gathered the information you need to register from your ISP (or intended website host), you can still reserve the name. The ISP and hosting information will not be required until you are ready to put the domain name into use. Reserving rather than registering the name costs an additional $49, on top of the basic $70 fee for a two-year registration. You can register a name for up to 10 years.

B. How to Check the Availability of and Register a Domain Name

NSI offers a quick way for you to find out whether a name is available, and if it is, to register it on the spot. Just go to www.networksolutions.com and type the name you want in the Register a Web Address box. Choose a top-level domain to the right (.com for most users) and click Go! If the name is available, you'll have an opportunity to also register the .net and .org versions of the same name if they're available (see Figure 2, below). Registration costs a minimum of $70 for a two-year period. Reservations cost an additional $49, for a total of $119.

Register a Web Address (domain name)

Search for a domain name – no obligation!

Need help to get started?

www. nolo   .com ⬍   Go!

1 enter a name, word or phrase   2 choose a domain   3 click Go!   **Click here.**

Web Address Search Results

Click to select each name you wish to register

nolo.com is not available.

Figure 1

Registration Options

Select the product that's right for you

Below are options for registering your Web Address (domain name). Choose one and click Continue.

ISP-hosted Web Address   [Continue]

● Technical information from your ISP or Web hosting service required to proceed

● $35 dollars per Web Address per year, payable by credit card. You can register for up to a 10 year term.

"Fast Track" Web Address   [Continue]

● No technical information required
● Secures Web Address immediately
● Includes dot com biz card™ or standard "under construction" page
● Access value-added services and special promotions from NSI
● $119 per address for first 2 year term, payable by credit card

dot com essentials™   [Continue]

● All of the above, plus:
● Business e-mail (myname@my-own-company.com)
● FREE listing in the dot com directory™
● $169 per package for first 2 year service term, payable by credit card

Figure 2

Search WHOIS

Search for Web Address, NIC handle, or host IP:

```
webvan.com
```
[search]

To use Whois, simply type in your search string with the appropriate keyword, for example:

- To look for a domain name, just enter the domain name, for example:"example.com"
- To look for a handle, enter, for example:"handle WA3509"
- To look for a nameserver IP, enter, for example:"host 121.23.2.7"
- To look for a name, enter: "name lastname, firstname" or "name The Sample Corporation"

```
Registrant:
Intelligent Systems for Retail, Inc. (WEBVAN3-DOM)
   1241 East Hillsdale Blvd., #210
   Foster City, CA 94404
   US

   Domain Name: WEBVAN.COM

   Administrative Contact, Technical Contact, Zone Contact:
      Network Administrator  (AN156-ORG)   netadmin@ISRWORLD.COM
      650.524.2200
Fax- - 650.524.4801
   Billing Contact:
      Billing, Network  (BN93-ORG)  netbilling@ISRWORLD.COM
      650.524.2200
Fax- - 650-524-4801

   Record last updated on 31-Mar-1999.
   Record created on 29-Jun-1998.
   Database last updated on 27-Jan-2000 15:33:46 EST.

   Domain servers in listed order:

   DINA.WEBVAN.COM                    216.33.224.3
   SCR02.SEC.DNS.EXODUS.NET           209.1.235.120
```

Figure 2 (continued)

If your name is taken, you may be interested in NSI's WHOIS search service, which gives you information about the registrant of any domain name registered with NSI. Say, for example, you have chosen *Webvan, Inc.,* as the name of your grocery delivery business and want to use webvan.com as your domain name. However, you soon discover that someone else has already taken this domain name. You run the name through the WHOIS search engine on the Network Solutions home page and find that Intelligent Systems for Retail, Inc., is the domain name registrant (see Figure 3, below). The search results also give you a contact name, phone number, address and email address. From there, you can decide whether you want to contact Intelligent Systems for Retail, Inc., perhaps to make an offer to buy the name. (Chapter 5 discusses more options if your chosen name is not available.)

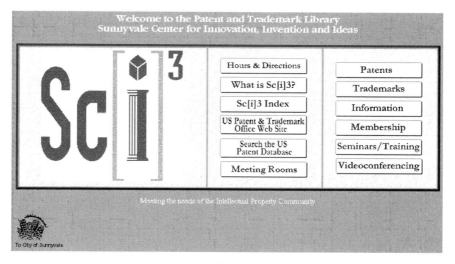

Figure 3

C. What to Register

In addition to your product or service name, you may want to register one or more related names, if they are available. These might be common misspellings of the primary name, names of specific product brands owned by your business and names that reflect the generic nature of your products. For instance, *Peet's Coffee & Tea* owns not only peets.com, but also coffee.com. Peet's might want to lock up petes.com (for the bad spellers), petescoffee.com and peetscoffee.com. (See Chapter 4 for more on how to choose a great domain name.) ■

When Your Domain Name Is a Trademark

If you are doing e-business on your website, or using the website to advertise goods or services you offer in the "real world," your domain name is also a trademark. Simply put, a trademark is any device that distinguishes your product or service from others in the marketplace, or designates their origin. For instance, say Jonah Ishmael creates an online art gallery that features and sells whale art by various artists. The art gallery is called *Jonah and the Whale* and resides on a website with the domain name ahab.com. Jonah is using ahab.com as a trademark because it is used to bring visitors to his commercially oriented website. Jonah is also using *Jonah and the Whale* as a trademark for the particular product being offered on the website—whale art.

Here are some examples of domain names that are also trademarks:

- Amazon.com (online retailer of books, CDs, toys and other items)
- Drugstore.com (online pharmaceuticals sales)
- Nolo.com (online legal information provider and publisher and retailer of legal books, forms and software).

A domain name isn't always a trademark. If ahab.com were a personal, noncommercial website with pictures of Jonah's family, poems he writes from time to time and a statement of his political philosophy, the domain name would not be a trademark. This is because the term ahab wouldn't be used to identify goods or services or an entity doing business on or off the Web.

Also, if a domain name is the same name by which the product or service is typically described, the law will consider it "generic" and won't treat it as a trademark. For instance, the domain name drugs.com uses a word that is the generic term for a class of products. As we point out in more detail in Chapter 4, generic names like drugs.com may make fabulous domain names but will most likely never receive protection as a trademark because the law does not allow monopolies over generic terms.

A. Your Rights As a Trademark Owner

Why should you care whether or not your domain name is a trademark? Because as the owner of a trademark, you have legal rights that may be very important for your business. If you're the first person or business to actually use a trademark in connection with the sale of goods or services, you are the "senior user," and you have priority in case of a conflict with a later user. This is true whether or not you've registered the trademark with the U.S. Patent and Trademark Office.

Example: *Peter develops software for taking orders over the Web and launches the sale of his Bearware software online. He uses the mark Bearware prominently on his website and as his domain name, bearware.com. Peter makes his software available for purchase online under the mark Bearware and through the domain name bearware.com on February 1, 2000, so that is the date of first use for purposes of trademark seniority. Gail develops similar software and also plans to market it under the trademark and domain name Bearware.com. But Gail doesn't offer her software for sale until March 1, 2000.*

Because Peter was the first to use the mark Bearware to sell his software, he is the senior user. If Gail sues him for trademark infringement, he will win the right to continue using the mark for selling his software and as his domain name.

If you're the senior user, you can go to court to prevent others from using your trademark—as a domain name or otherwise—if the use would likely cause customers to confuse someone else's product or service with yours, or to be confused as to the origin of the product or service. (See Chapter 7 for more on what constitutes customer confusion.)

Example: *Gail decides to sell her software under the Bearware mark over the Internet, but she uses the domain name bareware.com. Peter can sue Gail for trademark infringement, asking the court to stop Gail from using the*

Bearware mark and the barewear.com domain name. Peter will make a number of claims:

1. *He is the senior user of the mark Bearware.*

2. *Gail's use of the same mark to market and sell her software product (which is similar to Peter's) and her use of a domain name that sounds exactly like Peter's trademark are likely to cause customers to confuse her product and website with Peter's.*

3. *Gail's use of the same mark as Peter's for a similar software application is likely to cause customers to mistakenly believe that both applications come from the same company.*

B. Trademark Registration

Trademark ownership in the United States is based on who is first to use the mark (the senior user). But you can strengthen your ownership by registering a mark with the United States Patent and Trademark Office. This same rule applies to domain names that serve as trademarks—that is, domain names that are used as addresses for commercial websites. Generally, you can federally register a trademark if it is:

- used in interstate or international commerce (which includes virtually all commercial domain names)
- distinctive to some degree (that is, memorable in some way)
- not scandalous or immoral (four-letter words are verboten) and
- not likely to create customer confusion when compared with other registered marks.

The primary benefits of federal registration are that you are presumed to be the owner of the mark throughout the whole country, and anyone who infringes your mark will be presumed to have done it willfully. Infringement means you can collect large money damages, and possibly attorneys' fees, in a federal court lawsuit. Also, you are entitled to use the "r in a circle" notation next to your name to inform the world of your mark ownership. Unregistered marks are identified with the less powerful "™."

Chapter 8 explains the rules and benefits of registration in more detail and provides step-by-step instructions for filing a registration application on the Web.

For a more complete treatment of these and other trademark issues, see *Trademark: Legal Care for Your Business & Product Name,* by Stephen Elias and Kate McGrath (Nolo), or visit the Patent, Copyright and Trademark section of Nolo's free Legal Encyclopedia at www.nolo.com.

PROTECTION FOR UNREGISTERED TRADEMARKS

State Trademark Registration Laws. You can register your trademark with your state, but there are few practical benefits. State registrations were more important when it was common for marks to be used solely within a single state, which meant they didn't qualify for federal registration. However, with the advent of the Web, very few marks are now restricted to a state's geographical borders, and federal registration is definitely the preferred approach.

State and Federal Unfair Competition Laws. Trademarks that have not been federally registered can still receive certain kinds of limited protection under state and federal unfair competition laws. These laws bar other businesses from using your trademark in confusing and unfair ways. Protection from unfair competition is most useful when another business is trying to use your trademark to create the impression that its business is affiliated with yours. In other words, unfair competition laws can help you if someone isn't making it clear that they are not connected to your business.

For more on unfair competition, see *Trademark: Legal Care for Your Business & Product Name,* by Stephen Elias & Kate McGrath (Nolo).

C. Making a Domain Name a Strong Trademark

A distinctive domain name gets more legal protection as a trademark than a non-distinctive one does, and is usually more effective in the marketplace. The law grants distinctive domain names used as trademarks greater power to ward off copiers, for three reasons:

Distinctive names are memorable. The more distinctive a trademark is, like Yahoo!, the greater impression it makes on the customer's memory. This strong impression makes it more likely that a similar trademark, say Yoohoo.com used as a Web portal, will remind the customer of the original trademark. Needless to say, that can lead to confusion. Customers may think Yahoo! and Yoohoo are the same brand, or that they are related. They may mistakenly type in yoohoo.com instead of yahoo.com and go to the wrong website. They may be misled into thinking the reputation of one applies to the other. In either case, the rightful owner of the Yahoo! trademark may lose traffic, ad sales and profits.

Similar names are likely to confuse customers. The more distinctive a domain name is, the more likely it is that potential customers will assume that all products and services carrying that name originate from one source. For instance, it's reasonable to assume that all insurance-related services that carry the QuoteSmith mark, as in Quotesmith.com, originate from one company called QuoteSmith. You wouldn't make the same assumption for several quote services that use "value" in their names. The greater the likelihood that customers will associate a product or service carrying a particular name with a particular source, the greater the need to protect them against the confusion that would likely result if another business used the same or a similar name.

The business probably invested time and money to come up with the name. The more time, money and creativity that go into making a domain name distinctive, the more sense it makes to provide the mark with adequate protection. And if the distinctiveness comes from widespread customer recognition over time, it also makes sense to protect the business goodwill that has been built up under the mark.

To come up with a domain name that will serve you well as a trademark, follow these rules:

1. Use a name that's memorable or clever.

2. If you use a name that isn't distinctive, promote it so that it acquires a meaning in the marketplace.

3. Avoid conflicts with names that are already famous.

These strategies are discussed in Chapter 4. ■

How to Choose a Great Domain Name

To help your Web business flourish, you want to pick a domain name that will:

- be easy for Web searchers to find
- help market your product or service
- serve as a strong trademark, so competitors won't be able to use it or something similar, and
- be free of legal conflicts with other trademarks.

This chapter explores strategies for meeting these sometimes contradictory goals.

There's one consideration you can't get around: Domain names are limited to 26 characters, including the .com part. If you try to register or reserve a name that is too long, you'll be directed to provide a shorter version.

A. One Website, Many Domain Names

It's an unfortunate but inescapable fact that a domain name that satisfies one of the goals listed above may sabotage another. For example, a domain name that gets lots of people to your website quickly may make a crummy trademark. Take coffee.com; it may be an excellent domain name, because many people who are looking for coffee vendors online are likely to type the word coffee into their browsers. But coffee.com wouldn't qualify as a trademark for a coffee-related website, because the word coffee in that context is generic—it describes the product itself. So if your website were named coffee.com, you wouldn't be able to do much about goodcoffee.com, blackcoffee.com, columbiancoffee.com or cupofcoffee.com. But if you named your coffee website something like javadelights.com, you would have an easier time of chasing away anything that was similar in sight, sound or meaning. Coffee.com or javadelights.com? What a choice.

Fortunately, you can have the best of both worlds—you can claim several domain names and route them all to a single website. In fact, you can have an unlimited number of domain names leading to your unique website. This is because underneath every website lurks a set of numbers (your Internet Protocol, or IP, address) that identifies your unique location on a particular Internet server. Your Internet service provider can set up a system that routes multiple domain names to your IP address, and so to your website.

The only factor limiting how many domain names you can use to bring users to your particular website is cost. NSI currently charges $70 to register a domain name for a two-year period, so registering ten domain names would cost only $700, a modest amount for many Internet startups.

Because Internet users vary in how they seek out goods, services and established businesses on the Internet, the more bases you cover the better. So the owners of a coffee-related website might, as an example, register cupofcoffee.com, coffeeyumyum.com and cupofjoe.com as well as javadelights.com.

Another way to leverage a domain name is to create variations by adding words to the front of it, with another dot. For example, if you were using www.jelly.com and wanted to promote the New England jams and jellies you were selling, you could also use www.Vermont. jelly.com, www.Maine.jelly.com or NewEnglandjelly.com and so on, without registering additional domain names. These domain names could link to specific parts of your website; your ISP could set it up for you.

You're free to create as many variations like this as you can think of. Just be sure to add another dot when you add to the name. The domain name www.Vermontjelly.com (without the dot after "Vermont") would be a completely different domain name from www.jelly.com, and you would have to register it separately.

A potential downside to this strategy is that some folks may forget to include the extra dots when entering your domain name in their browser, and as a result will get a "no server found" message. If they take the time to error-check, though, they should be able to figure it out.

B. If You're Already in Business

If you are launching a website as part of an existing business, you must first decide whether you want to use the name of your business for at least one of your domain names. Most businesses do. That's why you'll find apple.com, landsend.com, toysrus.com and so on.

The importance of a strong brand on the Internet can't be overstated. Strong national and global competition for products and services online demands strong branding and a correlation between brand and domain name in order to get customers to the right website.

For example, say you are looking for the website of Peet's Coffee & Tea, a well-known coffee supplier. Rather than use a search engine to hunt for sites related to the terms "coffee" or "tea," you probably would first just type "peets.com" into your browser. Your guess would be right, and you would go right to the Peet's website. Had Peet's not used its brand name for its domain name, you would have been at least temporarily diverted from your search. And if you share the general lack of patience of many Internet users, you might have given up. By using its strong brand name for its domain name, Peet's can rest assured that anyone looking for the brand will quickly end up at its website.

Using the company name for your domain name also allows you to keep whatever goodwill you have built in the name. Goodwill simply means the good relationship you have with your customers because you provide exceptional service or a truly wonderful product.

You may decide, however, that a short, catchy and easy-to-remember name is a good alternative (or addition) to just using your existing business name. For example, the Collin Street Bakery in Corsicana, Texas, sells fruitcakes and has for many years—but when it came time to go online, the owners chose fruitcake.com as their domain name.

Still another option is to use only part of your business name, or an abbreviated form of it, as your domain name. (You're limited to 26 characters total, remember.) For example, Turners Outdoorsman, a retail sporting goods store, uses turners.com; Motley Fool (investment advice) uses fool.com, and Kelley Blue Book (wholesale and retail prices for used cars) is kbb.com. Ask Jeeves, a well-known search engine, uses ask.com. Short domain names are generally preferable to long ones, because many Internet users type the domain names into their browsers rather than relying on their list of favorite or bookmarked sites, portals (Yahoo!, AOL), or special interest sites that offer collections of links for parents, seniors, investors or other groups.

Of course, you may want to use another name altogether (like the bakery that chose fruitcake.com), especially if your business name is long. For instance, a well-known bookstore chain in Northern California called A Clean Well-Lighted Place for Books uses bookstore.com as its domain name. And Finer Times Market Place, an antique dealer, uses classicwatch.com.

As mentioned, generic domain names make weak trademarks because they merely describe the goods or services offered on the website (for example, healthanswers.com, drugstore.com, coffee.com), but excellent domain names because they work to get people to the website. So, depending on how well known your existing business name is, it may make sense to use two names. Create a new and descriptive domain name, and use your existing business name both as a second domain name and to sell goods or services on the website itself. The rest of this chapter gives more tips on choosing a good name.

C. Generic Names

A generic term can make a great domain name, because lots of people are likely to find your site. That's why domain names such as wine.com, furniture.com, pets.com and books.com were snapped up long ago.

As a general rule, generic domain names work best when you can use the actual term without modifiers or additional syllables. For instance, cars.com, drugs.com or coffee.com are the strongest and best uses of these generic terms. Domain names like fastcars.com, coffeebeans.com or bestdrugs.com aren't going to bring as many people to your site as the bare term would, but they're still considered generic for trademark purposes, meaning you get the worst of both worlds—an ineffective domain name and no trademark protection, either. If someone has got there ahead of you and is already using a key term by itself, consider adopting a classically distinctive domain name—that is, a name that is coined, arbitrary, fanciful, suggestive or flat-out clever. (See Section E, below.)

If you're considering a generic domain name (and someone else hasn't grabbed it yet), think it over before you decide to go with that name alone. As mentioned, having a generic name can certainly make it easier for people to find you on the Web. But because the name is generic, you probably will not have any trademark protection, and the U.S. Patent and Trademark Office probably won't register it. If you want to register your domain name as a national trademark, it must be distinctive enough to distinguish your product or service from others in the marketplace. For example, if a business names its new soft drink "Cola" and its website cola.com, it won't be able to register "cola" as a trademark. That's because "cola" describes a group of carbonated soft drinks with cola flavoring; it could refer to any of several brands of colas. But add "Shasta" to "Cola," and shastacola.com qualifies as a trademark because it specifies one particular brand of cola on the market. Other examples of terms that have always been generic are lite beer, super glue, softsoap, matchbox cars and supermarket.

D. Ordinary or Common Names

Many excellent domain names are made up of ordinary words. Consider taxprophet.com. Nothing remarkable about either tax or prophet, but put them together and you have a name with considerable cachet. Another example, Webvan.com, is the website of a grocery delivery service. There is nothing unusual about the words, but their combination is clever because it makes you wonder what is being delivered and piques your curiosity.

But what about trademark protection for a name consisting of ordinary terms? Here are the basic rules:

- If the overall name is distinctive, it will be protected as a trademark no matter how many ordinary terms are used.

- You cannot claim ownership to the ordinary terms themselves, but only to the overall name. For example, the owner of howstuffworks.com won't own "how" or "stuff" or "works," but will own the entire name.

- If the ordinary terms are memorable in the context of the product or service (for instance, Apple in the context of computers), the name will be considered distinctive. Common terms that consumers have come, over time, to associate with the underlying product or service will also be considered distinctive—for example, bestbuy.com for retail electronic products.

1. The General Rule: Little Legal Protection

On a scale of one to ten for trademark protection, generic names rate a zero, while distinctive names are a ten. In between are all sorts of names that aren't usually distinctive by themselves, but aren't generic either. This "ordinary names" category includes:

- names that use common terms in a standard arrangement—for example, healthanswers.com for, you guessed it, online health information
- place names such as DowntownNews.com
- personal names—for example, www.troweprice.com for T. Rowe Price investment funds; castlelaw.com for the Castleman Law Firm
- words that describe the product or service, such as i-courthouse.com for an online court that resolves disputes and allows Web surfers to serve as jurors; stampfinders.com, a full-service exchange for stamp collectors; and cleanswell.com for a website that sells household cleaners, and
- words of praise, such as bestpetshop.com (unless it becomes distinctive over time, as in bestbuys.com).

Misspellings or alternative spellings (such as "lite") cannot make an ordinary term ("light") distinctive. The same is true for common foreign language equivalents, like "le" for "the" and "casa" for "house." As a result, bestpetshop.com predictably will get little legal protection as a trademark. By contrast, a fanciful domain name like petopia.com is distinctive and easily protected as a trademark.

2. Protection If the Name Becomes Well Known

If an ordinary name becomes associated in the public mind with a product or service, the name can become a distinctive and legally protectible trademark. This is called the "secondary meaning" rule. Many famous and effective trademarks, like McDonald's or The Yellow Pages, originally consisted of ordinary terms that, over time, became widely recognized as product and service identifiers and so were transformed into strong marks. From its humble beginning as an ordinary mark, McDonald's has turned into one of the strongest marks in the world.

Similarly, when it first hit the market, the name Ben & Jerry's for a brand of ice cream was not distinctive and not entitled to much protection. However, as the Ben & Jerry's company advertised its products and as the products became well known (actually, adored) among the nation's ice cream buffs, the Ben & Jerry's trademark grew in distinctiveness. Now, the mark is highly distinctive as a brand of upscale ice cream— and the company's website is named, of course, benandjerrys.com. Other examples include schwab.com for Charles Schwab, Christies.com for auctions, sportingnews.com for the well-known sports periodical, and etrade.com for online stock trading.

Using a mark that can't be protected until it has acquired a secondary meaning can present a serious problem to your small business. You must accept the fact that the mark will be weak, and subject to possible use by others, until its reputation has been built up. If you can spend a lot of money to promote the mark when it's first used, you may be able to speed up the process of public recognition.

E. Distinctive Names

Distinctive, memorable domain names can make a strong impression on customers and are legally strong trademarks, easier to protect against use by others than are generic or ordinary names. They make customers think, "That's clever," or "Gee, I wonder what that means?" A product or service name can be distinctive for a number of reasons, including:

- The name is coined (made up)—for example, flooz.com, datek.com or multex.com.

- The combination of words and letters in the name is so creative that no one else has come up with it—for example, think360.com for services using cutting-edge three-dimensional photographic techniques.

- The name carries a clever double meaning—for example, google.com is an online search site; google is a word used by mathematicians to describe numbers beyond the trillion range. Another example: Pangea, a bioinformation company, uses doubletwist.com for its domain name, suggesting the famous double-helix structure of DNA.

- Certain words in the name are completely arbitrary in the context of the underlying product or service, as in online retailer Amazon.com; rhino.com, the website of Rhino Records; fool.com, the site for the Motley Fool investment advice firm and dogpile.com for search services.

- The name as a whole cleverly suggests the product without describing it, as in lendingtree.com for loans, hungryminds.com for online education, magicaldesk.com for secretarial services, medscape.com for health services and bottomdollar.com for a shopping site.

F. Creating a Distinctive Domain Name

George Eastman, the founder of Kodak and a man with an eye for a good trademark, could have been talking about domain names when he suggested that trademarks should:

- be short
- be vigorous
- be easily spelled, and
- mean nothing.

Some other good advice is to make your domain name:

- pronounceable
- memorable, and
- legally available (see Chapter 5).

The key to creating a distinctive domain name is cleverness. Coined words such as Exxon are the ultimate in clever because they are created from thin air. But you don't need to make up new words to have a distinctive name. As we have seen, distinctive names often consist of ordinary words used creatively and in an unusual context or words that evoke fanciful associations. You may also want to use ordinary words that indirectly suggest what the underlying product or service is, without describing it outright.

While it may seem that all the good names have been taken, there is in fact a large supply. But like diamonds, they usually aren't just lying on the ground for the taking; a little mining, cutting and polishing may be required to find them and make them shine. Some possible sources:

- new combinations of existing words such as ubid.com for auctions, smartmoney.com for personal finance calculators, buyitnow.com for a retail site
- combinations of word roots, like intelihealth.com for health services, bibliofind.com or alibris.com for book finding services, travelocity.com for travel services, invesco.com for investment services
- distinctive foreign words such as Sirocco.com or Soleil.com
- abandoned names that are no longer in use, but that were once famous. They may bring a certain cachet to your product or service if their image corresponds to the one you want to project. If you do discover a name you know was in use at one time, find out whether or not it is now available for your use by doing the sort of search described in Chapter 6.

> **FINDING UNCLAIMED MARKS**
>
> One online subscription service claims to have an inside track to domain names that were not renewed after their two-year registration expired. The service provides a list of these recently expired registrations on a weekly basis for a $20 subscription fee. While we don't endorse this service or provide any guarantees, such a list might provide a fruitful source of domain name ideas. You can reach the service at www.unclaimeddomains.com.
>
> If you do decide to use one of the names on this list, make sure that the name isn't still being used as a trademark on or off the Web. As with other domain name choices you may make, you should definitely subject your choice to a trademark search, as described in Chapter 6.

1. Coined Words

The best way to make a mark distinctive is to make it up. Some examples include chumbo.com (an online software store), kagi.com (a payment processing service for e-commerce businesses) and pandesic.com (an e-commerce company). The keys to a coined domain name are making it easy to spell and appealing to both eye and ear, or at least suitable to the image you want to project for your product or service. To avoid coined words that may evoke unintended images (for example, runslo.com for software that is supposed to speed up your Internet access), run your choices by a variety of people and note their responses to the sound and appearance.

Wholly new, made-up words have no meaning and probably not even any connotation, other than the ones you will create with your marketing activities. That means they require extensive, often expensive, marketing efforts to get established as product or service identifiers in the first place. Without that, your domain name won't mean anything to the general public. That's a major drawback for a small business with limited capital.

Opting for a coined word has a second drawback. New combinations that sound and look good—that is, ones that are marketable and not already in use—are becoming harder to develop. Despite our rich Celtic, Anglo-Saxon, Norman and Latin linguistic heritage, with over 200,000 new trademarks being registered each year, the well of coinable words is fast being drained.

2. Names That Suggest, But Don't Describe

In general, marketing folks favor suggestive names because they evoke an image or idea that customers are likely to associate with the product or service being marketed. A name is usually considered suggestive when you need to take at least one more mental step to figure out what is being suggested. Here are some examples:

- ask.com, the domain name for the Ask Jeeves search engine, effective because it suggests answers, just what you want a search engine to do
- peapods.com, the domain name for the Pea Pods baby things site, suggests maternity things
- peapod.com, a website featuring online grocery ordering
- Salon.com, an online magazine, suggests a place for the exchange of sophisticated commentary
- eHow.com, information made available in a crisp "how to" format
- Travelocity.com, a travel services website, suggests travel and speed
- nextMonet.com, an online contemporary art gallery that suggests undiscovered great artists

- Gazoontite.com (for allergy information and supplies) that suggests the ritualistic and widespread use of the German "Gesundheit!" (health) when someone sneezes
- Getsmart.com, a debt consolidation and loan service, suggests the quality of savvy, something that folks who have debt problems may aspire to, and
- wingspanbank.com (a national online bank) suggests a far-flung presence, something innovative in the banking industry.

Although suggestive names may require some marketing to become broadly identified with a product, they are usually easier to promote than coined names because they already connote something you want to associate with your product or service. Some name consultants argue that suggestive names are the most useful because the images they evoke make them very effective marketing tools. But it may take lots of thought to come up with one that's appropriately evocative, suits your customer base and hasn't been taken. Again, test your ideas out on a number of people to see if they get the message you hope to send.

3. Fanciful Words

Fanciful names are fun to invent because you can use any term, or combination of terms, that do not in fact describe your service or product in any way. The trick is to think up a term that is interesting, memorable and somehow appropriate, without literally describing some aspect of your service or product. For example, Yahoo.com and ragingbull.com (stock market and investment information site) are both fanciful names that would be easy to protect as trademarks.

Clearly, consumer responses to these types of names are subjective and intuitive. If you create a fanciful or arbitrary mark, try to consider all the possible evocations that the name may have—and make the most of them.

4. Arbitrary Words

Words that are descriptive or ordinary when associated with one product or service can be very strong for another. For example, Apple.com is distinctive and legally strong as a trademark because apples have nothing to do with computers, but Swingsets.com for a site that sells children's play equipment is weak because it literally describes the product. Similarly, Facets.com is a distinctive name for an online clothing store, but would be mundane, ordinary and non-distinctive as the name for an online gem store.

5. Common Terms in Uncommon Arrangements

Ordinary words, in unusual arrangements, can make distinctive names. For example, Magicaldesk.com has weak components—magical and desk are both common terms, but combine them for secretarial services, and the entire name becomes more distinctive and therefore more easily protected.

When evaluating a phrase to see whether it's a strong or weak trademark, it is the overall impression that counts. The fact that some of the elements are ordinary won't matter if the phrase as a whole has an original ring to it. For example, Speedy Turtle Delivery Service is memorable for the contrast of speed and turtle. This makes it distinctive, despite the fact that Speedy Delivery Service without the Turtle would be purely descriptive and so a weak trademark. Especially if you shortened the entire business name to speedyturtle.com, you would have a very distinctive domain name.

G. Names to Avoid

There are two categories of names to avoid when selecting your domain name:

- Names that the PTO will refuse to register as trademarks, and
- Names that will be in legal conflict with existing trademarks.

1. Names You Can't Register As Trademarks

If you want to protect your choice of domain name as a trademark, you'll want to register it with the United States Patent and Trademark Office. (Chapter 8 tells you how.) The PTO will not register any of the following:

- Names that contain immoral, deceptive or scandalous matter (essentially, four-letter words)
- Names that disparage or falsely suggest a connection with persons (living or dead), institutions, beliefs or national symbols
- Names identifying a particular living individual (unless his or her consent is obtained) or a deceased president of the United States
- Names that have been taken by an organization that has been granted the exclusive right by statute to use the name, such the Boy Scouts and U.S. Olympic Committee
- Names that are misleading or just plain false
- Names that are primarily a geographic name or a surname, unless they have acquired a "secondary meaning," as has, for example, schwab.com.

2. Names That Will Conflict With Existing Trademarks

You should always keep an eye out for possible legal conflicts when choosing your domain name. Even if you already have a business and have taken the necessary steps to register your name with the county clerk (for sole proprietorships and partnerships) or Secretary of State (for corporations or limited liability companies), you may violate someone's trademark by making your business name your domain name. Thousands of business owners have been stunned to discover that they can't use their chosen business name without running afoul of another business's trademark rights.

As a general rule, avoid domain names that are:

- Close to an existing domain name that is both distinctive and used on a competing website.

- The same as or very similar to a famous commercial name used online (Amazon) or off (McDonald's, Disney). Truly famous names get special protection even if use by someone else wouldn't confuse customers. Under laws known as "dilution" statutes, courts can stop any use of a famous name that is intended to trade off the strength of the name, or that has the effect of tarnishing the trademark's reputation for quality.

- The same as or confusingly similar to the name of a famous living person such as Michael Jordan, Julia Roberts or Hillary Clinton.

In addition, if all of the following four statements are true, you run at least some risk that you'll end up on the wrong end of a dispute over your domain name:

- Another business is already using your proposed domain name as its trademark.

- The other business's mark is distinctive, even if marginally.

- The other business started using the mark in actual commerce before you started using your proposed domain name, and

- Either the proposed domain name itself, or the products or services to be sold on your website, would create a likelihood of customer confusion. ■

What to Do If Your Domain Name Is Already Taken

Has the domain name you want already been grabbed by another business? Don't worry; you have options.

A. Use .net or .org

If you are like most businesses, you want .com at the end of your domain name. However, many .com names are unavailable, although the same choices may be available with .net or .org.

The availability of .net or .org is probably small consolation to you. E-commerce businesses often refuse to settle for .net or .org because .com has become, as it was intended to, uniquely associated with commercial activity. If you are one of these .com holdouts, you'll just need to keep plugging away with proposed names until a .com version is available.

If, however, your intended activity involves fostering access to the Internet (perhaps as an Internet service provider) or building a real or virtual organization of some type (as a nonprofit organization, for example), .net or .org may be just fine. In some cases, it may even be beneficial. Take the nonprofit national public radio and television entity, the Public Broadcasting Service (PBS). PBS, which derives its credibility and reputation for independent programming and news reporting from its nonprofit status, chose www.pbs.org for its domain name. By staying away from .com, PBS sent the message that the content on its website is non-commercial, which is appealing to those who support it.

Using .net or .org doesn't necessarily shield you from claims of trademark infringement. For instance, Amazon.com recently sued Amazon.gr (.gr is for Greece) for trademark infringement. However, a federal court has ruled that a domain name that ends with .net conveys a non-commercial purpose, which may reduce the likelihood of customer confusion between a .net site and a .com site. (If you want to read the judge's decision, you can find that case, *Avery-Dennison v. Sumpton*, at http://caselaw.findlaw.com/cgi-bin/getcase.pl?court=9th&navby= case&no=9855810. See Section D, below for more on trademark infringement.)

NEW CHOICES COMING SOON

In the not-too-distant future, there should be a greater choice of domain names, including:

.stor, for e-commerce sites

.firm, for business or professional sites

.web, for Web-oriented sites

.arts, for art-related sites

.rec, for recreational sites

.info, for sites providing information services, and

.nom, for sites supported by individuals.

B. Change the Name Slightly

A domain name is reported as not available only if the *exact* name is already taken. For instance, if an availability search tells you that madprophet.com is already taken, you may find that "mad-prophet.com" or "madprophets.com" is available. So, if you are not wed to the exact form of your first proposed domain name, you can experiment with minor variations until you find an acceptable name that is available.

The fact that a slightly different name is available doesn't mean that you can or should use it, however. Using a domain name very similar to an existing one may result in trademark infringement—the violation of someone's trademark rights. If you're found to have infringed someone's trademark, a court could order you to stop using the name and pay money damages to the other domain name owner. The result would depend on whether:

- the name is actually being used on a commercial website, or
- the close similarity in names would be likely to confuse potential customers.

For example, a potential customer who sets out to access the original madprophet site but who mistakenly types in a dash will end up at your site. This may be a temporary diversion, or it may represent the loss of the other site's customer to you. Especially if you are offering competing goods or services, you will have created the exact type of customer confusion that the trademark laws have been designed to protect against.

If you're thinking about choosing a domain name that is only a slight alteration of another site's domain name, read Chapter 7 on customer confusion first.

C. Buy the Name

Domain names are bought, sold and auctioned like any other property. If the domain name you want is being used on an actively maintained commercial website, chances are slim the owner will sell it to you. However, if the name has been reserved but isn't being used, you may be able to get it for a price you can afford.

How much is a domain name worth? Most domain names don't sell for that much (though some exceptions are listed in "Big Sellers," below). At GreatDomains.com, the leading online domain name brokerage house, the average offer price is around $32,000, and the average selling price is $14,500.

That website provides an interesting discussion of how it ranks and appraises the value of the domain names it deals in. For a detailed discussion of how this particular brokerage appraises domain names, visit its website at www.GreatDomains.com. The most important factors are:

- the number of characters (the shorter the better)
- the market potential of the business to which the domain name is attached (for example, car.com is more valuable than camping.com because it reaches a broader market); and
- the use of .com, which is better than .net or .org for a commercial enterprise.

You can buy a domain name in a variety of ways. You can look in online classifieds, contact the owner directly and make an offer, make a bid on an auction website (ebay.com, for example) or go through an online domain name broker such as GreatDomains.com.

BIG SELLERS

Prices of some recent big-money transfers of domain names:

business.com	$7.5 million
wallstreet.com	$1.03 million
computer.com	$500,000
question.com	$175,000
internet.com	$100,000
drugs.com	$823,000
ForSaleByOwner.com	$835,000

If you are buying or selling a domain name through an online broker (like GreatDomains.com), the broker will likely supply all the necessary paperwork to legally transfer the domain name. If you don't use a broker, you or the other party to the deal must supply the purchase agreement. If it falls on you to come up with an agreement, consider adapting the sample agreement below.

If you use an online broker, here's how your transaction might work. First, you go to the broker's website. If you find a domain name you want, you submit an offer to the broker, who forwards your offer to the seller. The broker then informs you whether your offer has been accepted, rejected or there is a counteroffer. If your offer has been accepted, the broker mails you a purchase contract and detailed escrow instructions to sign. You pay no broker fees. The seller pays all the fees.

BEWARE OF CYBERSQUATTERS

If the domain name registrant appears eager to sell the name to you and the name is the same or similar to a mark you're already using, take a moment to reflect. It's now illegal, under federal law, to traffic in domain names in this manner. See Section D for a more detailed description of how the law works.

D. Assert Your Rights As Senior Trademark User

Read the rest of this chapter only if you:
- are already in business,
- use a distinctive name to identify your product or service, and
- want to use that name as your domain name.

If you already use your proposed domain name to market products or services, you may have the upper hand in a dispute with someone who's using the domain name. Under trademark law, the first person to use a mark in commerce is considered the owner (more on this in Chapter 3, Section B). So if you used the name to market your products or services

SAMPLE DOMAIN NAME TRANSFER AGREEMENT

Domain Name Transfer Agreement

_____ (Buyer)

and _____ (Seller)

agree as follows:

1. Seller assigns to Buyer all right, title and interest worldwide to the _____*[Domain Name]*_____ domain name, together with any goodwill associated with it.

2. Seller represents that Seller has full power to enter into and perform this Agreement.

3. Seller will promptly apply to Network Solutions, Inc. (NSI) to transfer ownership and management of _____*[Domain Name]*_____ to Buyer under current NSI procedures for modifying a domain record. Specifically, Seller will instruct NSI to change the billing name, technical contact and administrative contact for _____*[Domain Name]*_____ to ___*[new billing name, technical contact and administrative contact information]*___. Seller will provide the information and email messages, and execute documents, necessary to accomplish the transfer of the domain name.

4. Buyer will pay Seller $_____ upon confirmation that NSI has changed the billing name, technical

SAMPLE DOMAIN NAME TRANSFER AGREEMENT (CONTINUED)

contact, and administrative contact as specified in Paragraph 2. A current printout of a WHOIS query provided to Buyer by Seller will be sufficient evidence of the domain name transfer. Buyer will issue a check for the full amount made out to _____, and send it via overnight delivery service to Seller at the address below.

5. As a courtesy, Buyer will attempt to forward to Seller from time to time any misdirected email messages received through the _____ *[Domain Name]* _____ domain name. Seller recognizes that Buyer's hardware and the Internet itself may not always function perfectly, and that delays might be involved in forwarding the email messages. In no event will Buyer be liable for any lost profits, lost revenue, lost data or any form of special, incidental, indirect, consequential or punitive damages of any kind, whether based on breach of contract or warranty, tort (including negligence), product liability or otherwise (whether or not foreseeable), even if informed in advance of the possibility of such damages, for failure to deliver or timely deliver any email message.

6. This Agreement will be governed by the laws of the State of _____ *[Buyer's state]* _____ .

7. If any provision of this Agreement is held by a tribunal of competent jurisdiction to be contrary to law, the remaining provisions will remain in effect.

SAMPLE DOMAIN NAME TRANSFER AGREEMENT (CONTINUED)

8. This Agreement constitutes the entire agreement between the parties with respect to the ___*[Domain Name]*___ domain name. This Agreement may not be changed in any respect except in writing duly executed by authorized representatives of each of the parties.

Seller's Full Name

Buyer's Full Name

Seller's Signature

Buyer's Signature

Date

Date

Address

Address

before the domain name registrant started using its domain name, you can prevent another business from using the same mark if:

- the mark is nationally famous (laws against trademark dilution protect famous marks from use by others, even if there is no customer confusion—see Chapter 4, Section G2), *or*
- the use creates a likelihood of customer confusion (discussed in some detail in Chapter 7), *or*
- the other user is a "cybersquatter" under federal law.

1. Choosing a Strategy

If you are a trademark holder and want to challenge the use of a domain name, you will first need to decide on a strategy for going after the registrant. You have three choices:

- **Use the dispute resolution service offered by ICANN.** ICANN, the international nonprofit organization now in charge of domain name registrations worldwide, recently implemented a process called the Uniform Domain Name Dispute Resolution Policy, or UDRP. This administrative procedure works only for cybersquatting disputes—that is, when someone has registered your name in a bad-faith attempt to profit from your trademark. It is potentially less expensive (about $1,000 to $2,500 in fees) and quicker than filing a lawsuit (just 57 days to resolution).

- **File a trademark infringement lawsuit.** If you win, the court will order the domain name holder to transfer the domain name to you, and may award you money damages as well. A lawsuit is always an option, whether or not you pursue ICANN's dispute resolution process. We discuss infringement lawsuits in Section 3, below.

STRATEGIES FOR GOING AFTER SOMEONE USING YOUR TRADEMARK AS A DOMAIN NAME

	ICANN Dispute Resolution Procedure	Trademark Infringement Lawsuit	Cybersquatting Lawsuit
Lawyer needed?	No	Yes	Yes
Cost	Approximately $1,000 to $2,500	$10,000 and up	$10,000 and up
Time	57 days from date you file your complaint	Months if the case settles, years if it goes to trial	A month or two
Grounds for relief	Bad-faith registration of your name	Trademark infringement	Cybersquatting
Who can be challenged	Any domain name registrant	As a practical matter, only U.S. registrants	As a practical matter, only U.S. registrants
What you may win	The domain name you want	The domain name you want plus money damages	The domain name you want, plus money damages for post-November 1999 activity

- **File a cybersquatting lawsuit.** If you win, you can not only get the domain name you want, you may also win money damages from the cybersquatter.

2. The ICANN Dispute Resolution Procedure

ICANN's new dispute resolution procedure applies to virtually all domain name registrants. (Before ICANN acted, NSI, which had a monopoly on domain name registrations in the United States, had its own dispute resolution system, which handled disputes between its domain name registrants and trademark holders.)

a. What You Must Prove to Win

To win your case in the ICANN procedure, you'll have to prove three things:

- The domain name at issue is identical or confusingly similar to a mark that you own, whether or not the mark has been registered as a trademark in the U.S. or abroad,
- The registrant has no rights or legitimate interests in the domain name, and
- The domain name was registered and/or is being used in bad faith.

You must prove similar things to prevail in a lawsuit based on the federal Anti-Cybersquatting Consumer Protection Act, discussed in Section 4, below. The Anti-Cybersquatting Act is, however, as a practical matter, enforceable in the United States alone. The ICANN procedure, on the other hand, can conveniently be used against domain name registrants outside of the U.S. as well.

Here's a look at each of these three elements in more detail.

Domain name's confusing similarity to your trademark. You must assert that you own the mark because you were the first to use it or because trademark registration has given you the right to its exclusive use. You must also state that the domain name really is confusingly similar to your mark. (If you need help understanding customer confusion, see Chapter 7.) If the domain name at issue is preventing you from using your mark as your own domain name, the "identical or confusingly similar" test will probably be satisfied.

Registrant's lack of rights or legitimate interests in the name. To prove this element, you must show three things:

- The registrant has never tried to use the domain name (or a similar one) in connection with legitimate commerce, on or off the Web;

- The registrant was never generally known by the domain name, even if the name wasn't used in commerce as a trademark; and

- The registrant isn't using the domain name in any legitimate way. A legitimate use would, for example, consist of use on a non-commercial website that engages in satire or criticism. But the use would not be legitimate if the registrant's actual intent is to divert consumers from your website or business location, or to tarnish your mark by lessening its reputation for quality.

Registrant's bad faith. This one is really the flip side of the second item. The registrant has acted in bad faith if you can show any of the following:

- The registrant acquired the domain name with the intent to sell it back to you or your business in particular, or to a competitor of yours, for profit. This wouldn't apply to those who acquire domain names with the intent to auction them off to the highest bidder later, because the plan was not directed specifically at you.

- The registrant has a pattern of acquiring domain names with the intent to block their use by legitimate trademark owners. That is, the registrant is a true cybersquatter. (See Section 4, below.)
- The registrant is a competitor who acquired the domain name primarily to disrupt your business.
- The registrant is using the domain name to attract users to the website by creating customer confusion. (See Chapter 7.)

b. How the Process Works

Your first step is to choose a dispute resolution "provider," which is an organization approved by ICANN. So far, ICANN has approved just two providers. Each has its own supplemental rules for dispute resolution, so in addition to ICANN's procedural rules you must follow the provider's rules. You can check them out at the provider's website, listed below. These sites offer detailed discussions about how to navigate the process.

To begin your case, you send a complaint to the provider, setting out specific facts that prove the three elements discussed above. Check the provider's website for fee information. Who pays the fees and how much will vary depending on the circumstances and the provider.

After reviewing the complaint for completeness, the provider will send the registrant a copy of the complaint, along with directions on how the registrant can respond and within how much time. The domain name registrant can continue to use the name until the dispute is resolved.

The provider will usually issue a response based solely on the complaint and the response. Either party may go to court if the decision is not to their liking. However, if the decision is in your favor, you will get the domain name transferred to you unless the registrant promptly files a lawsuit to prevent it.

The ICANN procedure is still new, and there will no doubt be numerous changes to it; the rules may have changed by the time you read this book. Check out the resources listed below to get the most up-to-date rules.

CURRENT INFORMATION ABOUT DISPUTE RESOLUTION PROCEDURES

ICANN: www.icann.org. Go there for the most current information about the new dispute resolution process.

DomainMagistrate.com: www.DomainMagistrate.com. This site is operated by Network Solutions, Inc., to help people figure out how to use the new domain name dispute resolution procedures.

Dispute Resolution Providers: ICANN has named two organizations, called providers, to help resolve domain name disputes: the **World Intellectual Property Organization (WIPO):** http://arbiter.wipo.int/domains and the **National Arbitration Forum:** www.arbforum.com/domains/.

---

3. A Trademark Infringement Lawsuit

As the senior user of a trademark, you can bring a trademark infringement lawsuit against the domain name owner if your trademark is distinctive and the use of the domain name creates a likelihood of customer confusion. As part of this suit, you can ask the court to require the owner of the domain name to transfer it to you and you may also be able to recover damages and attorney's fees. Of course, going to court is time-consuming and may cost you more than you'll recover from the defendant. You'll want to carefully weigh the possible benefits against the costs.

Things can get confusing if the trademark you've been using isn't exactly the same as your proposed domain name. If it's almost the same, trademark law lets you maintain ownership. But you can lose your seniority if there are *significant* differences. For instance, in one recent case, a company that owned the trademark "The Movie Buff's Movie Store" registered the domain name moviebuff.com. Another company, which had been using the actual mark "moviebuff" on a CD-ROM containing movie information, was prevented from using moviebuff.com as a domain name. The "Movie Buff's Movie Store" mark had been in use before the other company started using moviebuff on its CD-ROMs. Who was the senior user of the moviebuff trademark? The U.S. District Court ruled that the company using "The Movie Buff's Movie Store" was the senior user because it had used that name before the other company used moviebuff. But an appeals court reversed, ruling that "The Movie Buff's Movie Store" was an entirely different mark than moviebuff, and ordered the "Movie Buff's Movie Store" company to surrender the domain name to the moviebuff company. (*Brookfield v. West Coast Entertainment Corp.*, 174 F.3d 1036 (9th Cir. 1999). You can read this case at http://caselaw.findlaw.com/cgi-bin/getcase.pl?court=9th&navby =case&no=9856918.)

Trademark: Legal Care for Your Business & Product Name, by Stephen Elias and Kate McGrath (Nolo), is a book that explains how rights to conflicting trademarks are resolved and what's typically involved in trademark infringement actions

Trademark Disputes: Who Wins, Who Loses & Why, by Stephen Elias, is a downloadable eGuide, available at www.nolo.com.

4. An Anti-Cybersquatting Lawsuit

If you own your name and find that someone or some business is holding it hostage as a domain name until you pay a large sum for it, you may be the victim of cybersquatting. You can sue to get your domain name—and possibly some money damages—under a 1999 federal law known as the Anti-Cybersquatting Consumer Protection Act. Because suits must be filed in federal court, you almost certainly will need to hire a lawyer.

Under the Act, cybersquatting means registering, trafficking in or using a domain name with bad-faith intent to profit from the goodwill of a mark belonging to someone else. It refers to the practice of buying up domain names reflecting the names of existing businesses with the intent of selling the names for a profit back to the businesses when they go to put up their websites.

THE ORIGINS OF CYBERSQUATTING

The practice that's come to be known as cybersquatting originated at a time when most businesses were not savvy about the commercial opportunities on the World Wide Web. Some entrepreneurial souls registered the names of well-known companies as domain names, with the intent of selling the names back to the companies when they finally woke up. Panasonic, Fry's Electronics, Hertz and Avon were among the "victims" of cybersquatters. Opportunities for cybersquatters are rapidly diminishing, because most businesses now know that nailing down domain names is a high priority.

a. Recognizing Cybersquatting

How do you know if a cybersquatter has your name? As a general rule, you should first see whether your proposed but unavailable domain name takes you to a legitimate website. Simply enter www. and the domain name in your browser.

If the domain name takes you to a website that appears to be functional and reasonably related in its subject matter to the domain name, you probably aren't facing a case of cybersquatting. However, you may have a case of trademark infringement, as described in Section 3, above.

But if your browser produces any of the following results, and you are a famous individual or are using your existing business name as your proposed domain name, you may have a case of cybersquatting on your hands:

- You get a "can't find server" message
- You get an "under construction" page, or
- You get a page that appears to have no relationship to the meaning of the domain name. For instance, if you type the well-known Nolo trademark WillMaker into your browser (www.willmaker.com), you get Shells' Ragtown Political Art Studio. (Yes, Nolo.com appears to have its own cybersquatter problems.)

Although each of these results suggests the possibility of cyber-squatting, there may also be an innocent explanation for the lack of a functioning website, especially if the website is still under construction. It's very easy and inexpensive to register or reserve domain names but more difficult to put up the actual website. You can reserve a domain name for two years, so the fact that a website is not up, even months after the name was reserved or registered, does not necessarily mean that the registrant doesn't have perfectly legitimate plans to have a website in the future.

Before jumping to any conclusions about a proposed domain name that is not available, contact the registrant. (See Chapter 2, Section B, for how to do this.) Find out whether there is a reasonable explanation for the use of the name, or if the registrant is willing to sell you the name at a price you are willing to pay.

Sometimes paying the cybersquatter is the best choice. Even though Congress has provided a remedy against cybersquatting, it requires a federal court lawsuit and, almost by necessity, lawyers. It may be a lot cheaper and quicker for you to come to terms with a cybersquatter than to stand on your rights and invoke the power of the federal court with its attendant costs and delay. Although you may be able to recover your costs and attorney fees if you win, there is no guarantee; it's completely up to the judge.

b. What You Must Prove to Win

If somebody else has already registered your business name or other mark as a domain name, you can sue the registrant in federal court to have the domain name transferred to you. To win, you'll have to prove all of the following:

- The registrant had a bad-faith intent to profit from your mark (see section c, below),
- Your mark was distinctive at the time the domain name was first registered (see Chapter 4 for more on what makes a mark distinctive),
- The domain name is identical or confusingly similar to your mark, and
- Your mark qualifies for protection under federal trademark laws (see Chapter 8)—that is, you were the first to use the mark in commerce.

You don't have to show that customers are likely to be confused. (This is different from a trademark infringement lawsuit; see Section 2 above.) This means you can sue the domain name registrant even if the website sells products or services that are completely unrelated to yours.

c. Bad Faith

To win a lawsuit based on the Anti-Cybersquatting Act, you must show bad faith on the part of the domain name registrant. This will not be easy. There is no bad faith if the person who registered the name had reasonable grounds to believe that the use of the domain name was a fair use or otherwise lawful. If a cybersquatter is able to show a reason for registering the domain name other than to sell it back to the trademark owner, then the courts will allow him to continue.

If you can answer yes to any of the following questions, then there may be no bad faith:

- **Does the domain name registrant have an arguable claim to the name because of the registrant's existing trademark rights?** There may be concurring uses of the same name that are noninfringing, such as the use of the "Delta" trademark for both air travel and sink faucets. Similarly, the registration of the domain name "deltaforce.com" by a movie studio would not tend to indicate a bad-faith intent on the part of the registrant to trade on Delta Airlines' or Delta Faucets' trademarks.

- **Does the domain name identify the registrant as an individual?** A person is entitled to his or her own name, whether in business or on a website. Similarly, a person may bear a legitimate nickname that is identical or similar to a well-known trademark, such as in the well-publicized case of the parents who registered the domain name "pokey.org" for their young son who goes by that name.

- **Has the registrant ever used the domain name in connection with the offering of goods or services?** If the registrant has a commercially sensible reason for using the domain name (other, that is, than selling it back to you), there is probably not bad faith.

- **Is the registrant legally using the mark on the website itself?** It's legal to make noncommercial or fair uses of others' marks online, such as in comparative advertising, comment, criticism, parody or news reporting. The mere fact that the domain name is used for one of these purposes would not alone establish a lack of bad faith.

Congress has also provided us with some indicators of the bad faith necessary to prove a cybersquatting charge. If the answer to any of the following questions is yes, the court may be inclined to find that the registrant is acting in bad faith, or did so when the domain name registration was made.

- **Is the registrant using the domain name to divert users from your site to another site where customer confusion is likely to result or your trademark's reputation for quality is harmed?** In other words, is the domain name being used in a way that negatively affects your website or the value of your trademark?

- **Has the registrant offered to sell the domain name to you without having ever legitimately used the domain name on a commercial website?**

- **Has the registrant provided false or misleading contact information to the domain name registry or failed to keep this information up to date?**

- **Has the registrant registered multiple names that are the same or confusingly similar to distinctive marks?** In other words, is there an apparent pattern of cybersquatting?

- **Is the mark in question famous or highly distinctive?** The more distinctive or famous the mark, the more the court is likely to conclude that the registrant acted in bad faith.

IT'S THE FACTS THAT COUNT

In one of the first cases decided under the federal anti-cybersquatting law, a court ruled that a business that had used another business's trademark as a domain name had acted in bad faith and was a cybersquatter.

In 1985, Sportsman's Market (Sportman's) registered the trademark Sporty's, which it used on its aviation products catalog. Ten years later, Omega Engineering decided to sell aviation products and registered the domain name sportys.com. Nine months later, Omega created a wholly-owned subsidiary called "Sporty's Farms" for the alleged purpose of operating a Christmas tree farm, and sold the sportys.com domain name to it. Sportsman's learned of the registration, sued to obtain the domain name for its own use and won in U.S. District Court. Sporty's Farms appealed the trial court's decision.

During the appeal, Congress passed the Anti-Cybersquatting Act, and the appeals court applied it to this dispute. The court noted that the particular facts in this case didn't mesh well with the criteria set out in the Act for determining bad faith, a necessary ingredient for a successful cybersquatting charge. However, the court also noted that the Act allowed it to go beyond those criteria and, under the unique facts of this case, found that Omega had acted in bad faith. Sportsman's got the domain name sportys.com. (*Sporty's Farm v. Sportsman's Market, Inc*, Docket Number 98-7452).

d. What You Can Sue For

Under the Anti-Cybersquatting Act, victorious cybersquatting victims can ask the court for an injunction against the cybersquatter, and for monetary damages.

Injunctive relief is a court order requiring the domain name registrant to transfer the domain name to the plaintiff. Injunctive relief is available whether the cybersquatting occurred before or after the Act took effect.

RECOVERING YOUR GOOD NAME

If a cybersquatter has registered your personal name—or a name that is "substantially or confusingly similar" to it—you can sue in federal court to have the name transferred back to you. However, you will have to prove that the domain name registration was done with the specific intent of selling it back to you or to a third party for a profit. As a general rule, this will only work for famous people and politicians, since it's unlikely that the name would be registered with an intent to make a profit unless it belonged to someone well known.

If you win your lawsuit against the cybersquatter, you are also entitled to recover three times the total amount of money you lost because of the cybersquatter, plus the profits realized by the cybersquatter from his or her illegal activity, plus your court costs. In exceptional cases, you can also be awarded attorney's fees. However, cybersquatting usually doesn't cause actual monetary losses (though it does cause you massive inconvenience). Nor does it generate profits, unless you paid the squatter. So, at your option, the Court can award you "statutory damages" of $1,000 to $100,000. Since statutory damages do not require proof of any type, they offer you a realistic opportunity to recover money as well as the domain name.

Importantly, money damages (both actual and statutory) may only be recovered for cybersquatting activity that occurred after November 29, 1999. For instance, if the cybersquatting activity complained of is the registration of the name, and the registration occurred before November 29, 1999, you can't recover money damages. However, you can recover for other prohibited activities that occurred after November 29, 1999. For example, even if the domain name was registered before November 29, 1999, you can still recover money damages if the domain

name was trafficked in (for instance, offered for sale) or used after
November 29, 1999.

IF YOU CAN'T FIND THE CYBERSQUATTER

You may run into trouble when you try to sue a cybersquatter, because
you don't have a physical address to which to send the documents (a
complaint and summons) that get the lawsuit started. A lawsuit
generally can't begin until the person or business is properly notified
that it's being sued. And you can't send that notification by email.
Some cybersquatters provide inaccurate contact information to the
domain name registration service, making them next to impossible to
track down.

If you can convince the court that you've been diligent in trying to
locate the cybersquatter, but have failed to do so, the court will order
the domain name registration to give you the name. This is called an "in
rem" action.

■

CHAPTER 6

Making Sure Your Domain Name Doesn't Conflict With Another Business's Trademark

If your domain name is the same or very similar to another business's trademark, the trademark owner may someday (maybe someday soon) force you to stop using the name. Only by doing a search can you be reasonably assured that you have a legal right to use your proposed domain name. This chapter explains how to do your own search on the Internet or how to hire and use a trademark search service.

There are actually two elements you need to consider when determining whether or not your domain name may violate someone else's trademark rights. The first question, which you can answer with a trademark search, is whether your domain name is identical or very close to an existing trademark. The second issue is whether or not your use of the domain name would confuse customers, damaging the trademark owner's business or reputation. Deciding whether the simultaneous use of two similar trademarks is likely to create customer confusion is not always easy. (Chapter 7 discusses how to make this assessment; a consultation with a trademark attorney also may be wise, especially in close cases.)

For example, suppose you decide to start a Web-based business auctioning small antique collectibles such as old watches, jewelry and figurines electronically and at discounted prices. Your location in part of the San Francisco Bay Area called the East Bay prompts you to seek the domain name Ebaybuys.com. You search to see if the domain name is available from NSI and you find out it is available. You then surf over to the PTO's website, where you conduct a search of the PTO's registered and pending trademarks database using the instructions in Section C, below. You find the name Ebay is registered to Ebay, Inc., and that Ebay, Inc., is using the domain name ebay.com to auction antiques and collectibles as well as other types of goods.

The names Ebay and Ebaybuys obviously differ, but they may be close enough to confuse people. Because you also auction antiques, consumers might go to your website when they really wanted to go to Ebay's website. Or they might think that you are affiliated with Ebay because your domain name also uses "Ebay" as the root. This potential for consumer confusion means you are probably in danger of infringing Ebay, Inc.'s, trademark.

Be wary of search offers. Lots of banner ads on domain-name related websites offer services, including trademark searches. There is only one free trademark database available on the Web—the one offered by the U.S. Patent and Trademark Office and described in this chapter. Any other type of search is likely to cost you. It may be worth your while to pay for a competent search, but read this chapter before signing up. It may be that the service will charge you for the kind of search you can easily do yourself for free.

A. What Is a Trademark Search?

You want to engage in a systematic hunt for any trademarks that are the same or similar to your domain name. If you find such trademarks, you'll need to determine (with the help of Chapter 7) whether or not using your domain name would likely confuse customers.

There are three main categories of trademarks to search:

- Registered trademarks—trademarks that have been registered with the U.S. Patent and Trademark Office (PTO)
- Pending registration trademarks—names for which applications for registration have been filed with the PTO and are pending further action, and
- Unregistered trademarks—trademarks that are being used in commerce but aren't pending or registered.

B. Should You Do It Yourself?

There are three ways to conduct a trademark search. You can:

- Do it yourself using free online databases.
- Hire a search service or an attorney to do it for you.
- Do some of it yourself and hire someone to do the rest.

The third approach may give you the best legal protection for your time and money. Using your computer to search for registered trademarks on the PTO's website can be quick, easy and can provide good preliminary information. But before you actually put any serious money into building and marketing your own website, it would be wise to put your choice of domain name through a more thorough search for both registered and unregistered marks. You can also do this more rigorous search yourself if you are willing to climb a moderate learning curve. (See Section D, below.) Or, you can hire a trademark search service to do it for you. Count on paying roughly $200 to $400 per name. There are some things that a search service can do more efficiently (and often more inexpensively) than you can do for yourself. (See Section E, below.)

C. How to Do Your Own Trademark Search on the Internet

Searching for registered or pending trademarks on your own by using the PTO's online trademark database is easy. A typical search takes only about 15 minutes. You can make best use of your time by downloading the PTO's help file and studying it before starting your search.

This search allows you to compare your proposed domain name with registered trademarks and trademarks that are pending registration with the PTO. The results you come up with will include a list of the trademarks that meet your search parameters, and the names, addresses and contact information for the owners of those trademarks. You'll also learn how the trademark is being used (on what products or for what services) and what "international class" (category of goods or services) the mark has been assigned to by the trademark owner or applicant. This information is key in deciding whether you can go ahead and use the name without creating the likelihood of customer confusion. (See Chapter 7 for more on the international trademark classification scheme and why it matters in cases of apparent conflict.)

MEET TESS

As we were shipping this book to the printer, a new search system, called TESS (Trademark Electronic Search System) appeared on the PTO's trademark website, right below the now "older" system described in this chapter. The PTO plans to maintain both search systems for the immediate future, and the older system should continue to be sufficient for your needs.

Still, you may want to give TESS a try. It offers several features that aren't available on the older system:

- The "browse dictionary" option allows you to enter the name you are searching and see all the marks that appear before or after that name in the PTO's alphabetical list of trademark files.
- The Structured Form Search, while similar to the Boolean search described in this chapter, provides a larger number of options for structuring your search request. For example, in TESS you can search for two terms that are near each other or right next to each other. In the older system, you are limited to searching for terms that are located in the part of the trademark record you are searching.
- TESS not only reports marks that are registered or pending, but also marks that are, as TESS puts it, dead. A mark is considered dead if its registration was cancelled by the PTO or abandoned by the applicant.

TESS is the system that the PTO trademark examiners use. It is both powerful and flexible, and you may become confused if you aren't up to speed. You will do well to stick close to the online help as you search.

⚠ **Before you launch, get an in-depth search.** The step-by-step instructions in this chapter are limited to how to do a free search on the Web for registered and unregistered trademarks likely to conflict with your proposed domain name. For most people this level of search is just fine as a first step, but this chapter doesn't pretend to teach you the many tricks of the trade used by skilled trademark searchers. Before investing a lot of time and money promoting your website under your chosen domain name, you will be wise to conduct a more intensive search or pay a pro to do it for you. (See Sections D and E, below.)

1. Go to the Trademark Database

The first step is to go to the PTO's website at http://www.uspto.gov/ tmdb/index.html. You'll see the page shown below:

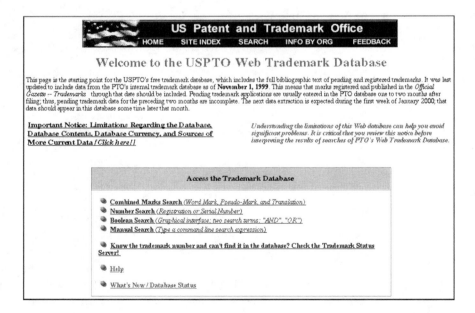

2. Choose the Type of Search

There are four different ways to search the database. The PTO provides online help, which is pretty good, along the way.

According to the PTO's Help file, the easiest option is the Combined Trademarks search. However, we disagree (respectfully, of course). All things considered, we think you are probably better off starting with the Boolean Search option. It provides the same basic choices as the Combined Trademarks search but adds a level of flexibility that makes it easier to search the database.

3. Select the Database to Search

You can search just for registered trademarks, just for pending trademarks, or for both. For most purposes, you'll want to search for both categories. After all, if a trademark is pending, you will have to pay as close attention to it as if it were already registered. Further, if you already own a trademark (because you were the first to use it) that you think conflicts with a pending trademark, you can initiate what's known as an "opposition" to prevent the registration. An opposition is a formal proceeding conducted by the PTO that is similar to a trial; you'll probably need a lawyer. (See Chapter 9.)

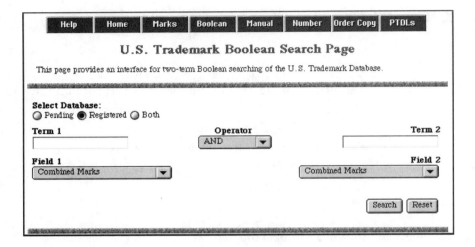

4. Formulate Your Search

The heart of all trademark searching is choosing the correct terms to search. Here are some tips for making the most of your trademark search.

a. One Term or Two?

With a Boolean search, you can look for one or two terms, which you enter as Term 1 and Term 2 on the screen. You may need to search for only one term. For instance, if your proposed domain name is MandalayLemonPies.com, you might want to search only for the word "Mandalay," the distinctive element of your name. If so, you would enter that word as Term 1, leave the Term 2 box blank, and then click Search. Or, if you wanted to search for all trademarks containing the term "lemon pie," you could enter that exact phrase—surrounded by quotation marks—as Term 1 and conduct your search.

You can search for more than two terms. If you want to formulate a search that uses three or more terms, you can start with the Manual Search option instead of a Boolean search. It works the same way as does the Refine Search procedure, which is explained in Section 6 below.

b. Using Operators

If you enter terms in both the Term 1 and Term 2 boxes, you'll need to pick what's called an "operator" to connect them. You can choose among the operators AND, OR and ANDNOT.

If you select AND from the pull-down menu of operators, you are telling the search engine to pull up all trademarks that contain *both* of your search terms. For example, the search query "shark AND talk" will produce every trademark that contains both the word "shark" and the word "talk." It will not produce a trademark that doesn't have both words.

If you enter these same search terms, but select the OR operator (making your query "shark OR talk"), your search will produce a list of all trademarks with the word "talk" and all trademarks with the word "shark." Needless to say, that list would be very long, because so many trademarks are likely to have the word "talk" in them. However, this approach can be very useful if your proposed domain name contains two distinctive words and you want to review every trademark that has either word.

For instance, suppose you're considering the name AnalogAstromaps.com for a website featuring a series of star charts. You would most likely want to use the OR operator to search for any trademarks containing either "analog" or "astromaps." Any trademark with either term might knock out your proposed domain name if the context showed a likelihood of customer confusion.

The third operator—ANDNOT—is not nearly as powerful as the AND and OR operators. You can use the ANDNOT operator to exclude from the search results any term you enter as Term 2. For instance, you may decide that you want to see every trademark with the term "astromap" but no trademark with the term "starchart." This search query would look like this: astromap ANDNOT starchart.

There is actually one more operator, but it's rarely used. The XOR operator lets you search for any trademark that has either Term 1 or Term 2, but not both. For example, if you searched for "analog XOR astromap," your search would turn up trademarks with either "analog" or "astromap," but not trademarks that contain both terms. There is seldom a reason to exclude a combination of two terms—indeed, in this example, the combination would be the most important trademark to retrieve.

c. Focusing on the Most Distinctive Terms

Focus on the part of your domain name that is most distinctive, because it is that part of your name that would most likely cause consumers to confuse your name with an existing trademark using that term. For instance, if your proposed name is zoroasterdesigns.com, the word to use in your search is "zoroaster," since it is by far the more distinctive of the two words. "Designs" is a generic word that can be used in a lot of different trademarks without creating customer confusion. So although you should search for any mark that contains either designs or Zoroaster, you are primarily interested in Zoroaster. You would not want to search just for "zoroasterdesigns," because it is very unlikely that that particular word would show up as a registered or pending trademark. (And if it did, a search for "designs OR zoroaster" would turn it up, anyway.)

It is also wise to go a step further and search for marks that contain one or more of the distinctive syllables in your name. For example, if you want to use bioscan.com, you might want to look for trademarks that contain either "bio" or "scan," because you might turn up something similar like "biosearch" or "cellscan." But it wouldn't make much sense to search for marks containing syllables that wouldn't likely be used. For example, the syllables "gazoon" and "tite" are not nearly as likely to be used in existing marks as are "bio" or "scan."

Don't use the .com in your search. Even though you are looking for a possible conflict with your domain name, which probably ends with a .com, don't enter the .com in the search engine. Although an increasing number of domain names are being registered as marks, complete with the .com, it is the other part of the name (to the left of the dot), that will create any likelihood of confusion, and thus a trademark conflict. Adding a .com to your search will very likely produce a report that overlooks important marks you need to know about.

d. Searching for Phrases

You can use two or more words as a single search term. All you need to do is enclose the phrase you're searching for in quotation marks. For example, a sensible search for Mandalay Lemon Pies would consist of searching for both Mandalay and the phrase Lemon Pies. You would do this by entering Mandalay as Term 1 and "Lemon Pies," (including the quotation marks), as Term 2.

e. The Truncated Words Feature

When you search for a particular term, it's useful to also search for slight variations of the term—for instance, if you are searching for the word "saber," you'll want to know about trademarks using the British spelling, "sabre." The computer won't find these variants for you without special instructions.

Fortunately, it's easy to get the computer to search for slight variations. One of the options offered by the PTO's Boolean search is what's called "right truncation." Right truncation allows you to chop off as much of the right-hand portion of a word as you wish and have the computer search for all words that start with what's left. For instance, instead of wondering whether to search for "sabre" or "saber," you could search for all trademarks which contain the root segment "sab." This would pull up both variations of "saber," but would also produce unrelated terms, such as "sabbath." To create this truncation effect, simply put an asterisk at the end of the string of letters that you want to search, as in "sab*."

f. Searching for Sound-Alikes

In addition to searching for names that are similar to yours in appearance, it is also important to search for words that sound alike. For example, gazoontite.com and gesundheit.com don't look that much alike, but they sound identical and might well confuse customers.

5. Choose the Part of the Database to Search

After you enter your search terms and choose the appropriate Boolean operator, there is one further step to take. For each term, choose which parts (fields) of the database you want to search. There are a number of choices here; the online help explains each field. We recommend the default field, which is "combined trademarks." Combined trademarks includes the literal version of all trademarks, registered or pending, and a slight variation on the trademark entered in the record by the PTO when the variation is common. For instance, if the trademark uses the word term light, the PTO may also add the word "lite."

TRADEMARK SEARCHING: A REAL-LIFE EXAMPLE

Bob and Steve have played tennis together for many years. When they hit their mid-fifties, one or the other would occasionally show up with a minor injury (sore shoulder, tender elbow) that dictated a change of pace in the game. They invented some special rules to make the game more easygoing when one of them needed a break. Bob and Steve started to laughingly refer to the rules—and the game they produced—as "Geezer Tennis." Aha, a good title for a humorous book. And perhaps the term Geezer Sports might be used on a line of books and other products for aging athletes, which could be sold on the Web at geezersports.com.

Steve checks with NSI and finds that geezersports.com is available for registration. He then decides to use the PTO's trademark database to do a trademark search, to see whether Geezer Sports is available as a trademark. He chooses to search for both registered and pending trademarks, and enters "Geezer" as Term 1 and "Sports" as Term 2. He selects AND from the pull-down menu of operators and leaves the pull-down menu for fields on "Combined Trademarks."

The search results show no registered or pending trademark using "Geezer Sports." Now what? Steve takes another look at the proposed trademark and realizes that the distinctive part of the name is "geezer," and that "sports" is a generic term. In other words, if there are other trademarks out there using geezer, Steve should know about them, even if they don't also use "sports." Steve performs another search, this time using "geezer" as Term 1 and leaving the Term 2 box blank. This time, the search turns up five trademarks that use the word "geezer."

One of those trademarks is *Geezer Golf*. Uh-oh. Steve clicks Geezer Golf and discovers that *Geezer Golf* was registered in three international trademark classes: 016 (Paper goods and printed matter), 028 (Toys and sporting goods) and 035 (Advertising and business services). This means that the line of Geezer Sports books that Steve and Bob had imagined would fall into at least two of the same classes as those for which Geezer Golf is registered. (For more information about the trademark classification system, see Chapter 8, Section D.) Using geezersports.com might well confuse customers about articles sold on

Bob and Steve's website and those identified by the existing trademark. (Customer confusion is discussed in Chapter 7.)

Bob and Steve are free to use geezersports.com as a domain name, because nobody else has claimed it. But because the name is so similar to a trademark that is being used in connection with similar types of products, the public might well be confused. This means that Bob and Steve probably couldn't get the name registered with the PTO—and even if they did, they might be sued for trademark infringement.

Alas, Steve and Bob give up on "Geezer Sports" but continue to enjoy their tennis rivalry. Maybe they'll come up with another clever name in the course of a particularly heated match.

6. Refine Your Search

After you get your results from a PTO search, you'll have an opportunity to refine your search. You can modify your search, either to broaden it if you received too few results, or to more narrowly focus your search if you received too many.

Probably the most important feature of the "Refine" or "Manual" search options is that you can combine Boolean operators. For example, suppose your proposed domain name is MiracleMediations.com. Using the Boolean search option as a starting place, you enter "mirac*" as Term 1 (truncating the term with the asterisk, to also search for "miracle") and "mediat*" as Term 2 (truncation lets you search for "mediate," "mediation" and "mediator" as well as "mediations"). You choose the AND operator to search for trademarks that contain both terms (plus the variations taken into account by the asterisk).

This search is a good start, but as you review your search results you realize that you want to search for trademarks that contain the word "arbitration" as well. To do this, you create a new search query that looks like this: "ms/mirac*" AND "ms/mediat*" OR "ms/arbitrat*." This search expression tells the computer that you want all trademarks that contain a variant of the truncated term "mirac*" and either the term "mediat*" or the term "arbitrat*."

The ms/ that precedes the truncated terms is what's known as a field code. The Manual/Refine search requires the use of these field codes if you want anything other than a "Combined Marks" search (the default search represented by the ms/). For instance, if you want to search for all marks owned by a particular company, you can use the field code "on/" in connection with the company's name. Similarly, use of the field code "gs/" lets you search for all marks that are used on goods or services containing the terms you use in your search query. For more on field codes, use the table that appears on the Manual/Refine search page and click whatever field code you wish to know more about.

D. How to Search for Unregistered Trademarks

There is no list, anywhere, of unregistered trademarks as such. But by searching the Web, you can find product and service names that aren't registered trademarks but are still trademarks being used by other businesses. As the percentage of businesses marketing their goods and services on the Web approaches 100%, the ability to discover the real-world use of unregistered trademarks improves apace.

A good place to start is the Dot.com Directory at www.dotcomdirectory. com/nsi/basic.hm, a comprehensive listing of business websites. Simply enter the name of the product or service that you're looking for, and you will obtain a list of sites that have such products or services. This list may include some currently used commercial names that are the same as or similar to the one you want to use. Another good place to search for unregistered trademarks on the Web is the Thomas Register of goods and services, at www.thomasregister.com.

Finally, you can simply enter the name in one of the Web's many search engines and see what turns up. Although this type of search will produce all uses of the term, not just instances of use as a trademark, it may still produce some useful information.

E. Using a Trademark Search Service

Specialized trademark search firms traditionally conducted searches only for trademark attorneys. Even today, some of the largest trademark search firms refuse to conduct searches for anyone but a lawyer. But most search firms aren't so choosy and will conduct a search for anyone willing to pay them.

1. Why Use a Search Service

Before putting a lot of time and money into promoting your website, you'll want to be as confident as possible that your domain name is "bulletproof" when it comes to trademark infringement claims. The free Internet search described in Section C is a good start, but commercial firms will give you a better idea of whether your name will survive a conflict with a pending or registered mark. Most businesses adopt a cost/benefit approach and hire a search service to do a final trademark search.

Here are some of the things a commercial search service can do for you:

Obtain a search report that is completely up to date. The PTO's website is always about two to four months behind. (The site tells you when the database was last updated and when the next update will be.) So if someone has filed an application to register a trademark very similar to your proposed domain name within the last few months, your search won't pick it up. A four-month lag time is tolerable to initially determine the legal viability of your proposed domain name, but you should definitely have an up-to-date search done before pouring money into promoting the domain name.

Search state (not just federal) trademark registration records. Every state allows the registration of marks that are used primarily in that state. If your choice for domain name is the same or confusingly similar to one of these state-registered marks, you may run into trouble if the mark's owner decides to use the mark for a domain name, only to discover that you have registered it first. So it's always a good idea to run your choice by the list of state trademark registrations, something a commercial service can do for you more efficiently than you can do for yourself.

Locate variations on and fragments of the distinctive part of your name. Sometimes similarity in sound or appearance of just a portion of two names is enough to cause customer confusion. Experienced searchers have a knack for spotting potentially troublesome fragments and will probably do a better job of finding them than you would.

Search proprietary databases for unregistered marks. Over the years, commercial search firms have built their own private databases of business and product names and logos. These firms also have access to, and are adept at searching, the many hundreds of commercial databases available through Dialog and other online aggregators of data. A search of these databases may produce conflicts that you probably would not discover in your relatively disorganized search for unregistered marks, whether you searched on the Web or in a library. Although most of these databases are available to the general public, you must pay either a subscription or one-time use fee, and learning to use them requires some effort.

Trademark: Legal Care for Your Product and Service Name, by Stephan Elias and Kate McGrath (Nolo), can give you a good start if you want to do your own comprehensive search.

2. Cost Factors

You can hire either a trademark search firm or a trademark lawyer to handle a search for you.

Because only attorneys are allowed to offer legal advice about potential trademark conflicts, trademark search services offered by attorneys tend to cost the most. If you hire a trademark attorney to advise you on the choice and registration of a domain name, the attorney can arrange for the trademark search. Some attorneys do it themselves, but most farm the search out to a search firm. Once the report comes back from the search firm, the attorney will interpret it for you and advise you on whether to go ahead with your proposed domain name.

Trademark search firms offer many different levels of services, and their fees vary accordingly. The price often depends on how much handling the information receives before it is delivered to you. Generally, raw data is cheap; highly processed and organized data is more expensive. For instance, if the search just involves running one proposed domain name past the PTO's database, the cost usually will be less than $50. But if you want the searcher to seek out registered trademarks that in whole or in part might resemble your name in meaning, sound and appearance, then the cost increases as the labor required does. If you also want the search to include an intensive hunt for unregistered marks, you are getting up into the several-hundred-dollars range.

The difference in rates among search firms may also reflect variations in the coverage of the search, the type of report you receive, the experience of the searchers or simply economies of scale. Some firms may advertise an unusually low price to draw in customers, but then add on charges that end up exceeding another firm's total price—a professional version of bait-and-switch advertising. To shop sensibly you need to know the total cost of each service, so be sure to ask questions before committing yourself. For example, does one fee cover the whole cost, or is there also a per-page charge for the report?

3. Finding a Service

There are many trademark search services in this country. You don't have to worry much about where a particular service is located—phone, fax and email make it possible for a customer in Bangor, Maine, to comfortably deal with a service in Austin, Texas. But if you want a local service, consult an electronic "Yellow Pages" such as those offered by Yahoo!, Netscape and the major search engines. Although some trademark search firms limit their services to lawyers, most also do searches for individuals and businesses.

Some trademark search services will try to convince you that you're stupid if you don't search every corner of the globe for possible conflicts. Don't just agree; make an independent decision about what scope of search is appropriate for you. Also, some search services provide additional services, such as the preparation of applications for federal and state trademark registrations. Like trademark lawyers, these businesses have a vested interest in convincing you that you will be better served by paying them to handle the tasks in question than by doing them yourself. If you feel that this point of view—which may in some cases be perfectly reasonable—is being too aggressively pushed in your situation, get a firm hold on your wallet and consider finding another service.

SILICON VALLEY SEARCHERS

California's Silicon Valley is home to the Sunnyvale Center on Innovation, Invention and Ideas, or Sc[i]3 (pronounced Sigh-Cubed). It is one of three Patent and Trademark Depository Libraries—the others are in Detroit and Houston—that have formed partnerships with the U.S. Patent and Trademark Office. Under this partnership, these libraries are encouraged to offer a variety of information services, including trademark searches, for very reasonable fees, usually a notch or two below those charged by commercial firms.

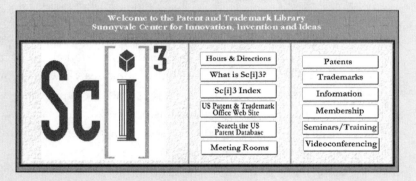

Sc[I]3 offers searches of varying scope. Like most trademark search firms, Sc[i]3 doesn't interpret its results; it leaves that to you. Your basic task is to review the trademarks that Sc[I]3 turns up in its search and compare them to your domain name for the likelihood of customer confusion. (Chapter 7 helps you do this.) You can order a Sc[i]3 trademark search by calling 408-730-7290. Visit www.sci3.com for a current list of services and fees. You can get the results of the search within 24 hours if you are willing to pay a premium. Otherwise it takes a little longer.

You may also find help with your trademark search by physically visiting one of the other 80-plus Patent and Trademark Depository Libraries located throughout the United States. These libraries usually offer excellent reference services for people doing their own research. Visit www.uspto.gov and click Libraries-PTDLs on the home page for a complete list of locations and contact information.

F. Assessing Your Search Results

Once you've carried out your trademark search, you'll have several options, depending on the results.

If your search turned up no results, your search parameters were probably too narrow. You should rethink your search strategy and try again. Although it's possible that no existing trademarks exactly match your proposed domain name, it's virtually impossible that there aren't some marks that are at least close.

If your search turns up trademarks that you think might conflict with your proposed domain name, your next step is to go to Chapter 7. You will be looking for the answer to one question: Would the use of your domain name create the likelihood of customer confusion between the products or services on your website and those identified by an existing mark? If you answer yes, you might well be guilty of trademark infringement if you go ahead and use the domain name you're considering.

If you conclude that your domain name won't infringe another business's trademark, your next step is to consider registering the domain name with the PTO as a trademark. We explain that process in Chapter 8. ■

CHAPTER 7

How to Tell Whether Customer Confusion Is Likely

You need to consider the issue of customer confusion if you have run your proposed domain name through a trademark search and found that a similar name—one that resembles yours in sound, appearance or meaning—is already being used by another business. Whether or not you should go ahead with your name depends on whether doing so would create a likelihood of customer confusion. If there is a likelihood of confusion, you risk being sued for trademark infringement if you use the name. If customer confusion isn't likely—for example, Delta Airlines and Delta faucets have coexisted peacefully for years—you can go ahead with the name.

If you're worried about infringement—yours or someone else's—the advice of an experienced attorney can be very helpful. Courts resolve trademark disputes on a case-by-case basis, and someone who has studied a variety of cases should have an informed opinion. See Chapter 9 for advice on how to find a trademark attorney.

A. What Constitutes Customer Confusion

The phrase "likelihood of confusion" is the key to most trademark conflicts. A "likelihood" means that confusion is probable—not necessarily that it has happened, or that it will happen, but that it is more likely than not that a reasonable customer would be confused by the simultaneous use of the two names.

Confusion in this context can mean two different things. Most commonly, it means that the goods or services a customer buys are different than what the customer intended to buy. For instance, suppose, on the recommendation of a friend, that you decide to purchase Lee's famous Flamebrain barbecue sauce, which is sold only on the Web. You intend to type "flamebrain.com" into your browser but accidentally enter "flamerbrain.com" instead. You get a website run by Henry, who has both copied Lee's idea to offer a barbecue sauce for sale on the Web and, with a very minor variation, the name of Lee's sauce. You order two bottles, completely unaware that you ordered the wrong product from the wrong website.

The other kind of customer confusion occurs when a misleading name causes customers to believe—wrongly—that a product or service is sponsored by, approved of or somehow connected with a business they already know about. In other words, customers are confused about the source of the product or service. This would be the case, for example, if you took your TV to a repair shop called IBM Electronics because you thought that IBM somehow sponsored the business.

The law imagines a "reasonable" customer who exercises ordinary care to distinguish among products and services. Courts recognize that a reasonable consumer will often make a snap judgment. For example, if, after only a hurried glance, you are confused between Heartbeat and Heartlite cooking oils, then the marks are too similar. That's reasonable. However, the law would surely not find it reasonable if you confused Heartbeat cooking oil with Esther's Cooking Oil because your Aunt Esther had recently died of a heart attack. Nor would you be reasonable in confusing Heartbeat with Esther's because of similar packaging, so long as the very different names were prominently displayed on the packaging.

Someone who alleges a trademark infringement must show (if the dispute goes to court) that a reasonable customer might be confused by the simultaneous use of the two marks. Typically, the challenger must somehow prove that a significant percentage of customers would likely be confused—anywhere between 5% and 50%, depending on the situation. The percentage varies from one court decision to the next. Proof typically comes in the form of statistically valid surveys and focus groups.

⚠️ **Watch your metatags.** Metatags are brief descriptions and key words that are pulled from a website's content and made part of the website's code. Users don't see this code, but it is visible to search engines. As a general rule, metatags should consist only of descriptive terms—ordinary terms that define your site's content—rather than distinctive terms that are in use by competing websites.

A court recently ruled that metatags that initially divert people away from a website containing a registered trademark may violate the trademark owner's rights. (*Brookfield Communications, Inc. v. West Coast Entertainment Corporation,* 174 F.3d 1036 (9ᵗʰ Cir. 1999).) If your metatags have this effect, you could be forced to change them.

For example, suppose Josh launches a website for buying and selling Pokemon cards. Pokemon is a registered trademark of Nintendo of America, Inc., which operates pokemon.com. If Josh uses the word pokemon as a metatag, he might run afoul of Nintendo's trademark rights and end up at the wrong end of a court order forcing him to get rid of the metatags and perhaps pay money damages to Nintendo.

B. Factors to Consider When Evaluating Potential Customer Confusion

Courts use a number of criteria to determine whether or not there's a likelihood of confusion between two names. If your domain name is very similar to an existing trademark, you will want to ask the same questions a judge would:

1. Are your goods or services closely related to those of the other business—that is, are they sold in the same marketing channels to the same general group of customers?

2. Do the goods or services compete—that is, will the decision by customers to buy one business's product or service be made at the expense of the other business?

3. Are the names very similar in sound, appearance and meaning?

4. Is the other trademark strong or distinctive?

5. Are the underlying goods or services expensive? How careful are people likely to be when deciding whether to buy them?

6. Does your business share the same customer base even if your goods and services aren't marketed in the same channels?

7. Does the other business use the name on several different products or services? Is it likely to do so in the future?

The first three factors are the most important. If none of them indicates a likelihood of confusion, you can probably stop there. In a borderline case, consider the rest of them.

This area of the law is unsettled. The issue of when a domain name infringes an existing mark is a new one for the courts. So far they have used the same basic criteria as those used for conflicts between other types of marks. However, the U.S. Supreme Court has yet to rule in a domain name case, and federal Courts of Appeal are just beginning to weigh in. Visit the Updates section of the Nolo website at www.nolo.com to check for significant new developments.

1. Are the Goods or Services Closely Related?

When similar names are used on related goods or services, the risk of consumer confusion is high. You can determine whether goods or services are related by asking these questions:

- Do they belong in the same class of goods or services?
- Do they pass through related marketing channels?

a. "Classes" of Goods and Services

The U.S. Patent and Trademark puts every new trademark in one or more "international classes," which are categories of goods and services.

There are 42 classes in all, 34 for products and eight for services. The Appendix contains a complete list of the classes and descriptions of each.

Goods or services within the same class are likely to be related either because they compete with each other or are marketed in the same channels.

Most commercial websites offer services, especially information services. Other examples of Web-based services are investing, auctions, entertainment and retail (for instance, Amazon.com provides a retail service even though it sells a wide variety of goods carrying their own marks). If your website offers information services (Class 42), and your domain name resembles a mark used by another information service provider, your domain name and the other mark fall within the same international class.

How can you tell what class the possibly conflicting mark belongs in? When you do a trademark search (described in Chapter 6), the search results will show what class or classes have been assigned to the marks the search turns up. If the goods or services offered on your website belong in the same class as those of the other business, this is a pretty good indication that the services will be considered related.

Example 1: *The owner of megasoft.com, a developer of downloadable software, wants to sue the owner of megasoft.net to stop megasoft.net from selling its custom-developed downloadable software. Both names fall into Class 9 for downloadable software. The owner who was first to use the mark for selling downloadable software would likely prevail if the dispute reached court.*

Example 2: *Software developer megasoft.com probably couldn't stop a maker of ultra-soft, custom-knit blankets, which are in Class 24, Fabrics, from using the name megasoft.net to sell its blankets over the Web. Downloadable software and blankets don't compete in any way; they are not considered related goods, and the megasoft mark could be used on both without creating the likelihood of customer confusion.*

By itself, the fact that two products or services are in the same classes does not conclusively establish that two names are legally in conflict. The classification system packs all goods and services into only 42 classes—combining, for example, abrasive cleansers and cosmetics—so products within the same class may be marketed in totally different ways so as to avoid customer confusion. You could certainly argue that a trademark for a scouring powder that is similar to a trademark for lipstick won't confuse customers.

To classify your own product or service, study the list of classes in the Appendix. The choice may be obvious; if it isn't, look at the examples for each class. If you are still not sure, pick the three most likely classes and use them as possibilities.

b. Marketing Channels

It is also useful to look at the marketing channels through which the goods or services reach the public.

The fundamental question here is whether customers are likely to encounter or learn about the different products or services in the same store, website, catalog, advertising or other means of promotion or distribution. If so, then they are more likely to think the goods or services are associated in some way. It is the likelihood of this type of confusion that could cause a judge to order you to find a different domain name. If, on the other hand, non-competing products are marketed quite differently, then no confusion is likely to exist, regardless of what class they are in for registration purposes. For instance, digital cameras and computers are non-competing products, but because they are both electronic products, they often show up on the same websites. Use of the same mark on these different products would still likely confuse customers as to their source, even if there were no confusion as to the products themselves. However, except in large warehouse-type stores such as Costco and Wal-mart, vacuum cleaners and basketballs seldom share the same commercial space, and the likelihood of customer confusion would be low.

The Web itself can be seen as one large marketing channel. However, such a view would make all products and services sold through the Web related, which in turn would instantly create a legal conflict between many thousands of trademarks that have been adopted and used in reliance on the "separate channel" analysis. As with so many issues arising from the intersection of trademark law and the Web, this one has yet to be squarely addressed by the courts.

Be conservative. Because the law in this area is so uncertain, we strongly advise you to be conservative. If your search turned up a similar mark or domain name, choose another domain name if the two names are distinctive to some degree (see Chapter 4), and customers would likely encounter both of them in pursuit of a particular product or service on the Web.

2. Do the Goods or Services Compete?

Goods and services directly compete if the purchase of one negatively affects the purchase of the other. If the goods or services offered on your website directly compete with goods or services identified by an existing mark, a court would probably find a likelihood of confusion if the existing mark is distinctive and your domain name is similar in sound, appearance or meaning to it. (See Section 3, below.)

3. How Similar Are the Names?

The third factor in determining whether using similar names will cause a likelihood of confusion is how similar the names are. Do they sound or look alike, and if so, how much? Do they convey the same meaning? The closer two names are in sight, sound and meaning, the more likely it is that a legal problem will arise. For example, trains4travel.com and trainsfortravel.com would obviously create confusion in the marketplace.

Even marks with greater differences may create the likelihood of customer confusion in the same market. Courts have found that Quirst is too close to Squirt, Sarnoff too much like Smirnoff, Lorraine too reminiscent of La Touraine. Each of these pairs of names were used on nearly identical goods. Probably the use of such close names would have passed legal muster if they had been on very different kinds of products. But the more that competitive names are in the same class or market channels, the less similar the names have to be to cause confusion.

The last four factors, though usually not as important as the first three, are sometimes significant.

4. Is the Other Trademark Strong?

You are safer in using a name that is similar to an existing weak trademark than one that is similar to an existing strong trademark. A mark is considered strong either because:

- the words, phrases, or symbols it consists of are distinctive (arbitrary, coined or suggestive), or

- long and continuous use has made the public recognize it as the symbol of a particular product or service (it has acquired a secondary meaning).

The weaker a name is, the less legal protection it is given, and the more likely it is that your domain name will be found to not be confusingly similar, even if it has many similarities.

Example: *New Legal Solutions, Inc., wants to use the domain name webdocs.com for its website, which offers electronic forms. However, a trademark search discloses that the term "Webdocs" is registered on the Federal Principal Trademark Register. New Legal Solutions is surprised at the registration, because Webdocs appears to be too descriptive to qualify for the*

Principal Register (see Chapter 8). New Legal Solutions decides to run a search for Webdocs on the Internet. The search engine returns hits for 150 different websites that use Webdocs for the same purpose intended by New Legal Solutions.

Because the term is in such general use, and therefore legally weak, New Legal Solutions decides to go ahead and use it as a domain name. The trademark owner may technically have an infringement claim against New Legal Solutions, but New Legal Solutions would have a strong defense, which is the mark's lack of distinctiveness due to its widespread use throughout the Internet. (Using the name, however, is probably not the best choice for other reasons discussed in Chapter 4.)

5. Are the Goods or Services Expensive?

Because customers tend to take their time and consider carefully when buying an expensive item, the more expensive the item, the less chance of confusing customers. An item that is cheap or likely to be bought on impulse, however, is more likely to result in customer confusion if it is sold with a mark that is similar to another on goods that are even slightly related.

6. Do Your Businesses Share the Same Customer Base?

Two businesses that use similar names to sell to the same customers are highly likely to cause customer confusion. But if businesses have separate customer bases, then the use of similar names is unlikely to confuse anyone. For example, the market for replacement wood windows is likely to be limited to contractors and homeowners with spare cash. As a result, a window manufacturer who uses the domain name WallsofLight.com and the same name in its advertising probably won't confuse the customers of a climbing gym supplier that calls its special demonstration the Wall of Lights. The two groups of customers don't overlap.

It's useful to look at how large a sector of the market uses your product or service. If a small sector of the market knows and purchases a service, a similar mark used by a different small group is unlikely to confuse the two sets of consumers. But if a large segment of the public knows one name, use of a similar name is more likely to cause customer confusion, even if aimed at a slightly different market, because of the greater potential for overlap between the two groups.

7. Is the Name Used on Several Different Products or Services?

A red flag should go up if the potentially conflicting name has already been used on a variety of products or services by the same business, even if you wish to use it on a product that is unrelated to any of these uses. An owner who uses the name on several products or services has what is called in legal lingo the "right of expansion." Some examples of businesses that do this are Calvin Klein and Pierre Cardin, who have expanded from clothing to fragrances, accessories and other products.

The rationale for this rule is that the public, having seen a name on a variety of goods made by the same company, is likely to assume that any new uses also belong to that company, and thus are likely to be confused. For example, the public would expect the name *Yamaha*, which already appears on motorcycles, lawnmowers and guitars, to represent the same company if it also appeared on computers or musical recordings.

Courts also assume that the first user may wish to expand the name's use further, and they protect this right of expansion by permitting very few other uses of the same name. So a second business seeking to use such a name, even on greatly dissimilar products, will have less luck than if the name were being used in a more limited fashion. ■

How to Register Your Domain Name As a Trademark

Being the first to use a trademark—not registering it—makes you the owner of a trademark. But registering your trademark with the U.S. Patent and Trademark Office will make it easier for you to enforce your legal rights as a trademark owner because it makes you the *presumed* owner of the trademark. If a dispute over the trademark arises, and a lawsuit is filed, it will be up to the other party to convince the court that you are not the owner.

In addition, once your mark is registered, every later user is presumed to know about it. Any infringement by them will be presumed deliberate, making you eligible for triple damages (three times the amount of money you actually lose as a result of the infringement), profits earned by the defendant as a result of the infringement, and possibly attorney fees. If you can't sue for these enhanced damages, you may well have trouble finding an attorney to take your case without a very large retainer fee. And if you can't find an attorney, you may well have trouble enforcing your rights as a trademark owner.

This chapter explains how to file your trademark application online. If you need more help once your application is filed, check the resources discussed at the end of this chapter.

A. Applying for Registration: An Overview

Filling out and filing a trademark application for your domain name with the U.S. Patent and Trademark Office is a snap. The PTO website offers two online application programs, called e-TEAS and PrinTEAS. According to the PTO, it shouldn't take you more than 20 minutes to complete the application.

The filing fee for registering most domain name marks is $325. It can go up if your website will be offering a number of different types of services.

To complete the registration process, you must actually be using the domain name on a website. However, you can start the application process on the ground that you intend to use the name in the near future (called an intent-to-use application). If you go on to actually use it and complete the registration process, your application date will also be considered the date of first use for the mark, which will give you a priority claim over later users. (See Chapter 3 for more on trademark ownership priorities.)

Although it's easy and quick to apply for trademark registration, the processing of your application can take a year or more. The PTO is overbooked and understaffed these days. In the meantime, your actual or intended domain name will appear in the PTO's trademark database as a pending trademark. Anyone doing a trademark search (see Chapter 6) will find your name and know that you are claiming it as a trademark. This in itself gives you a lot of protection because it will deter others from pursuing your name as a trademark.

B. What Domain Names May Be Registered As Trademarks

Not all domain names may be registered as trademarks. The PTO appears to be unwilling to register generic domain names, such as coffee.com or drugs.com. Similarly, the PTO will look askance at weak domain names, such as those using a surname or descriptive terms. (Chapter 3 discusses the difference between distinctive (strong) marks, descriptive (weak) marks and generic marks.)

Even weak marks, however, can usually make it on to what's called the supplemental register. So if the PTO rejects your original application because your mark lacks distinctiveness, you can amend the application and ask that the mark be added to the supplemental register. The supplemental register doesn't provide the same benefits as the main trademark register (called the Principal Register), but it does put your mark on the map, so people will find it when they do a trademark search. At the very least, you will prevent unknowing infringement of your domain name.

Federal rules prohibit certain types of trademarks from being registered at all. There haven't been any court decisions on how these rules apply to domain names, but existing trademark law suggests that the following types of domain names are not registrable:

- Domain names that contain "immoral," "deceptive" or "scandalous" matter. Immoral or scandalous, in this context, means that the mark might cause scandal or be disgraceful, offensive, disreputable, or excite retribution or elicit condemnation from the average consumer. These rather loose guidelines are considered in light of the mark itself and with the goods or services to which it is attached. There aren't any recently decided court cases on this subject, but you can imagine that some four-letter words with a .com after them are not going to be accepted by the PTO. A deceptive mark is one that suggests that the product or service came from a source other than its true source—for example, a domain name such as californiacheese.com, which only sells cheese from Wisconsin. (The PTO uses the sample of your trademark, which you are required to submit along with your application (called the specimen) to make sure that, among other things, your name is not deceptive. See Section D, Step 2, below for more about specimens.)

- Domain names that disparage or falsely suggest a connection with persons (living or dead), institutions, beliefs or national symbols. For example, the domain name jackieofashions.com would not be a registrable trademark for a website that attempts to use Jackie Onassis's image to sell clothing totally unconnected with the former first lady or her estate.

- Domain names that consist of or contain a name identifying a particular living individual (except with his or her written consent), or the name of a deceased president of the United States during the life of his widow, if any, except with the written consent of the widow. For example, you may be able to register the domain name barbrastreisand.com, but the PTO won't register it as a trademark for a website that sells Barbra Streisand CDs, photos, dolls, plates and other memorabilia, unless Barbra Streisand gives you written consent to use her name.

- Domain names containing marks that organizations have the exclusive right, by statute, to use. Boy Scouts is a good example. Similarly, use of the name Smokey the Bear is reserved to the Department of the Interior. So boyscouts.com and smokeythebear.com are off-limits as trademarks.

C. Different Ways to Register, Online and Off

The PTO now offers a quick and easy way to file a trademark registration application online. There are actually two systems available on the PTO website: e-TEAS and PrinTEAS. This book takes you through e-TEAS, which is a fully electronic system, allowing you to both fill in and file your application to the PTO online. PrinTEAS allows you to fill in the application online, but you must print out your filled-in application and send it to the PTO through the regular mail. If you decide to use PrinTEAS, you can easily adapt our instructions to fill in the application, and we provide instructions for mailing the application to the PTO.

Which program should you choose? It's faster and cheaper to use e-TEAS, because you don't have to pay for postage. One possible barrier to using e-TEAS, however, is the "specimen" requirement. If you are filing on the basis that you are already using the domain name (called an "actual use" application), you will have to submit a electronic file showing your domain name in actual use. (For more on specimen requirements, see Section D, Step 2, below.) This entails capturing your image in jpeg or gif format using a graphics program like *Adobe Illustrator* or *Photoshop*, *ImageStyler*, *AppleWorks*, *SimpleImage* or *Microsoft ImageReady*. If you don't have this type of software, or you are graphics-software challenged, you can always use PrinTEAS and accompany your application with a hard copy of your chosen specimen. There's one more wrinkle. If you are using a Macintosh computer, you will need *Netscape Navigator* to fully operate e-TEAS. Microsoft's *Internet Explorer* for Macintosh will not allow a proper image attachment. If you are filing on an "intent to use" basis, you won't have to worry about sending a jpeg or gif file.

If you want to fill out the application form on paper, you can download it from the PTO's website. If you prefer this method, you may want to use the instructions in *The Trademark Registration Kit* by Patricia Gima and Stephen Elias (Nolo).

D. How to Use e-TEAS to Register Online

Using e-TEAS can be fun. It sure beats trying to file the paper form. Just follow along with our step-by-step instructions below. If you need additional help, the PTO provides help links.

Step 1: Go to the PTO's website.

Your first step is to go to the PTO's website at www.uspto.gov. On the home page, click "Trademark." It will take you to the following page:

Patent and Trademark Office Home Page

Choose "Apply for a Trademark Online." That link takes you to this page:

Trademark Electronic Application System

The United States Patent and Trademark Office (USPTO) is pleased to present TEAS - the Trademark Electronic Application System. TEAS allows you to fill out an application form and check it for completeness over the internet. Using e-TEAS you can then submit the application directly to the USPTO over the internet. Or using PrinTEAS you can print out the completed application for mailing to the USPTO. It's your choice!

SPECIAL NOTICE:

On January 10, 2000, the filing fee for an application to register a trademark increased from $245.00 to $325.00 per class. Applications filed after January 9, 2000 will NOT receive a filing date unless at least $325.00 in fees is paid when the application is filed. See Office of Finance notices published in the December 7, 1999 *Official Gazette*, and the December 3, 1999 *Federal Register* at 64 FR 67774.

e-TEAS

The following special requirements apply for filing a trademark or service mark application directly over the internet:

- To file for a stylized or design mark, you must be able to attach either a black-and-white GIF or JPG image file (the only two formats currently accepted).
- To file an application based on use in commerce, you must be able to attach a scanned image or digital photograph in the GIF or JPG format of your specimen (sample) of actual use.
- You must pay by credit card (Mastercard, Visa, American Express or Discover) or through an existing USPTO deposit account. The filing fee is $325.00 per class of goods and/or services.

PrinTEAS

If you cannot file electronically, you may still be able to complete the application on-line, to print out and mail. But,

- You must pay by check or money order or through an existing USPTO deposit account (we currently cannot accept credit card payments using PrinTEAS). The filing fee is $325.00 per class of goods and/or services.

■ TEAS gives step-by-step instructions for completing a trademark or service mark application form properly. It also provides access to a wide variety of information about Office procedures and practice. While the different sections of the forms may appear straightforward and easy to fill out, you are strongly advised to read the HELP instructions very carefully for EACH section PRIOR to actually completing it. Failure to follow this advice may cause you to fill out sections of the form incorrectly, jeopardizing your legal rights.

■ e-TEAS works only if you use either NETSCAPE NAVIGATOR (Version 3.0 or most recent) or MICROSOFT INTERNET EXPLORER (Version 4.0 or most recent). e-TEAS utilizes frames, JavaScript, and the file upload feature supported by these browser versions. Note: Internet Explorer on the Macintosh platform will NOT permit a proper image attachment.

■ PrinTEAS, on the other hand, works best if you use either NETSCAPE NAVIGATOR (Version 3.0 or most recent) or MICROSOFT INTERNET EXPLORER (Version 4.0 or most recent).

■ For general trademark information, please telephone the Trademark Assistance Center, at 703-308-9000. For automated status information on an application that has an assigned serial number, please telephone 703-305-8747 or check our Trademark status server.

■ If you need help in resolving glitches or need answers to technical questions, you can e-mail us at PrinTEAS@uspto.gov. Please include your telephone number, so we can talk to you directly, if necessary.

■ PrinTEAS is available 24 hours a day, 7 days a week. e-TEAS, however, will NOT permit credit card payments from 11 p.m. Sat. to 6 a.m. Sun. EST. Applications will not transmit during that period.

■ You may wish to perform a search to see if there is a federal registration or pending application for a similar mark used on related goods and/or services. Please see http://www.uspto.gov/tmdb/index.html

⚠ Important Notice:
Once you submit an application, either electronically or through the mail, we will not cancel the filing or refund your fee, unless the application fails to satisfy minimum filing requirements. The fee is a processing fee, which we do not refund even if we cannot issue a registration after our substantive review.

e-TEAS

Click here to use e-TEAS !

PrinTEAS

Click here to use PrinTEAS !

E-TEAS and PrinTEAS Home Page

As you can see, you must choose between e-TEAS and PrinTEAS. If you scroll down the page, you'll find out which versions of *Netscape Navigator* and Microsoft *Internet Explorer* to use and how to contact the PTO for help.

Step 2: Click the e-TEAS link.

You will get the Form Wizard page, and will be asked some questions. Here is how to answer.

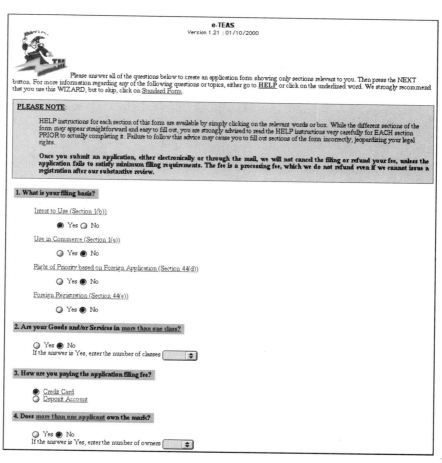

E-TEAS Form Wizard

Question 1: What is your filing basis? If you are already using the domain name on your website and selling goods or services, select "use in commerce." If you are not yet up and running, select "intent to use."

The procedures for each basis are somewhat different, and the "intent to use" basis will cost you an additional $100 when you do put the domain name into actual use.

Previous Foreign Registration. If you are filing in the U.S. on the basis of a previous foreign registration, see a lawyer before continuing. This book doesn't cover U.S. registrations based on foreign registrations.

Question 2: Are your goods or services in more than one class? The PTO categorizes trademarks in 42 different classes based on the goods and services the business offers. To see which classes your goods and services belong in, check the list of classes in the Appendix. You'll also find in the Appendix a PTO circular that discusses which classes are appropriate for certain computer-related goods and services ("Identification and Classification of Certain Computer-Related Goods and Services").

If the type of good or service being offered by your website clearly fits within one of the classes described by the PTO, go ahead and enter the class number in the blank. If you think you fit in two or more classes, you can use this application to register under the additional classes. The more classes you register under, the broader your protection is likely to be. (See Chapter 7.) However, you must pay a filing fee of $325 for each additional class. So if money is an issue, pick the best class and use that for your initial registration. You can always file applications for additional classes down the road.

If your goods or services do not match the descriptions given in the PTO circular, try checking the "Trademark Acceptable Identification of Goods and Services Manual" on the PTO's website. Just go to the PTO home page, www.uspto.gov, and click "Trademark." The next screen will show three columns. The first column is for trademark resources. Click "Trademark Acceptable Identification of Goods and Services Manual." The best way to use the manual is to use the search feature. Click "Search" and use keywords to find the list of goods or services that best describe your particular goods or services. For example, if you're going to use your trademark to identify your line of roasted coffee beans, type in "coffee" and click "Search" to find a list of coffee and coffee-related products from the Manual. This list will give you the PTO's suggested class number for your coffee beans. The PTO's list will also include descriptions, which you can use later on in the application.

If you can't choose a class, all is not lost. You can skip this part of the application, and the trademark examiner assigned to your application will contact you later with some suggestions. Who says government isn't friendly?

Question 3: How are you paying the application filing fee? This one is easy. You'll probably be paying with a credit card. Deposit accounts are usually used only by law firms and other businesses that register a lot of trademarks.

Question 4: Does more than one applicant own the mark? The applicant is the person or business that will own the trademark. If at all possible, only one person or business entity should own the domain name. This can be an individual, a partnership, a corporation, a limited liability company or a joint venture. If your situation dictates that there be two or more owners, click "more than one owner" and read the instructions.

Question 5: Is there one applicant, but more than one signatory? If there is a single applicant, only one person is needed to sign the application. If the applicant is a corporation, and corporate policy dictates that two or more officers sign the application, then enter the appropriate number here. If there is more than one applicant, then at least one person for each applicant must sign the application.

Question 6: Is an attorney filing this application? If you plan to be represented by an attorney in your dealings with the PTO, click "attorney." The PTO will not communicate directly with you if an attorney is representing you.

Question 7: Is the applicant's address outside the United States? If you live outside the U.S., click "applicant's address" for more information.

Step 3: Click "Next."

This takes you to the page shown below.

Trademark/Service Mark Application, Principal Register, with Declaration

eTEAS - Version 1.21: 01/10/2000

Each field name links to the relevant section of the "HELP" instructions that will appear at the bottom of the screen. Fields containing the symbol "*" **must** be completed; all other relevant fields should be completed if the information is known. If there are multiple owners or if the goods and/or services are classified in more than one class, click on the Form Wizard. **Note**: ☐ check here if you do not want the scrolling help to be automatically shown at the bottom of the screen.

Important: ONCE AN APPLICATION IS SUBMITTED ELECTRONICALLY, THE OFFICE WILL IMMEDIATELY PROVIDE THE SENDER WITH AN ELECTRONIC ACKNOWLEDGMENT OF RECEIPT OF THE APPLICATION. Please contact the Office within 24 hours of transmission (or by the next business day) if you do not receive this acknowledgment. Contact Points:

For general trademark information, please telephone the Trademark Assistance Center, at 703-308-9000. For automated status information on an application that has an assigned serial number, please telephone 703-305-8747, or use http://tarr.uspto.gov.

If you need help in resolving technical glitches, you can e-mail us at PrinTEAS@uspto.gov. Please include your telephone number in your Email, so we can talk to you directly, if necessary.

Applicant Information

Please use the Wizard if there are multiple applicants.

* Name	[If an individual, use following format: Last Name, First Name, Middle Initial/Name]

Entity Type: Click on the one appropriate circle to indicate the applicant's entity type and enter the corresponding information.

○ Individual	Country of Citizenship	
○ Corporation	State or Country of Incorporation	
	State or Country Where Organized	
○ Partnership	Name and Citizenship of all General Partners	
○ Other	Specify Entity Type	
	State or Country Where Organized	

E-TEAS Standard Application Form

Carefully read the information at the top of this page. The first block explains the help system and lets you turn off the help text that automatically appears at the bottom of the page. It also explains that only the blanks marked with an asterisk are mandatory. We strongly recommend that you be as complete as possible in your responses, even if the information isn't mandatory; it may save you time and trouble down the line. Some of the non-mandatory information may be useful to the examiner in evaluating your application and expeditiously communicating with you if a problem arises. For example, your phone number isn't mandatory—but how will the examiner call you if you don't include it?

The name, entity, address, email address, fax number and phone number blanks all come with excellent help should you need it.

Mark Information: Click the first circle above the words "Typed Format." Because you are registering a domain name, your trademark consists solely of words and numbers and will be displayed in what's called "typed drawing format." In the box just below the words "Enter the mark here," enter your domain name in capital letters. You can enter the complete domain name, including the .com, or just the unique part of your name. For instance, Nolo might choose to register its domain name as NOLO.COM or just NOLO. Because domain names are such a new species of trademark, there are no firm rules.

Additional Statement: This blank is optional, and you can safely skip it. About the only statement that might be relevant is what's called the disclaimer. This means that if you are using common, generic or descriptive words as part of your domain name, the PTO will want you to disclaim (give up) trademark rights in those specific words, even though you have a trademark in the name as a whole. For example, suppose you manufacture a highly successful line of perfume called Candor, and you wish to register the domain name candorperfume.com. The PTO will likely ask you to disclaim the word "perfume" because it is generic. The word "candor," however, is still registrable as a trademark for a line of perfume. That's OK since those generic words can't be registered or protected anyway. The trademark examiner will tell you somewhere in the process what words you should disclaim, so there is no point in doing it on the application.

Basis for Filing and Goods and/or Services Information: The information required in this part of the application will vary, depending on whether you are already using your domain name in commerce or are filing on an "intent to use" basis. The top part of this box shows you which type of application you are filling out: Section 1(a) Use in Commerce, or Section 1(b) Intent to Use.

Specimens: If you're filing under Section 1(a), use, you'll need to provide a specimen image file and a description of the specimen in the next box. If you're an "intent to use" applicant, you will not have a specimen information section on your application and should go to *International Class*, below.

Your specimen must be a file in jpeg or gif format. If you are registering your entire domain name, it should be a copy of your Web page showing your domain name. Or, if you are just registering the unique part of your domain name (without the .com), your specimen may be an advertisement of your services. Either way, make sure your specimen shows your name exactly as you described it in the "mark" box above.

Your specimen must show two things:

1) You are using your domain name as a trademark. A specimen that shows your website and the domain name typed into the address line of your browser is not sufficient. Your domain name should be a prominent part of the design of your home page. Ideally, it should be at the very top of the page, easy to spot and easy to read, and it should dominate the quadrant of the page in which it is located.

2) The services being offered on your website match the description of the services in your application. If you are providing financial information as your service, for example, make sure your specimen shows that you are doing so.

The next part of the specimen box asks you to describe what the specimen submitted consists of—for example, a digitally captured image of the home page where the goods or services are offered, or the front page of an advertisement offering the goods or services for sale.

International Class: Enter the number of the classification you selected for the goods or services offered on your website. (See the instructions for Question 1, above, for more on trademark classifications.) Or, if you prefer, you can send in your application without specifying a class and let the trademark examiner help you. If you want to register under more than one class, click "Form Wizard." This takes you back to the question where you are asked under how many classes you want to register. Once you enter a number other than "one" in that space and click the next button, you will be given a different application template that accommodates multiple classes.

Listing of Goods and/or Services: Here is where you describe the goods or services to which your domain name is attached. The good news is that you are only expected to make your best guess. A trademark examiner who doesn't approve of your description, or is confused by it, will let you know and work with you to come up with an appropriate description. If you don't feel like guessing, consult the "Trademark Acceptable Identification of Goods and Services Manual," a long list of goods and services that will help you come up with a proper description of the ones you plan to offer on your website. You can find it at www.uspto.gov/web/offices/tac/doc/gsmanual/manual.html#services. These descriptions are written up by the PTO, so you can copy them directly.

Trademark Acceptable Identification of Goods and Services Manual

Table of Contents

Goods

The **S** field indicates the status of the record: **A=added, M=modified, D=deleted**. The **Date** field indicates the date of that status. Minor corrections to an entry, e.g., typos, are not considered changes in status.

☞	IC	S	Date	Goods
☞	009	A	2/20/96	Abacuses
☞	010	A	4/2/91	Abdominal belts
☞	010	A	4/2/91	Abdominal corsets
☞	010	A	4/2/91	Abdominal pads
☞	001	A	4/2/91	Abrasive [indicate specific use or industry] (Auxiliary fluids for use with)
☞	001	A	4/2/91	Abrasive compositions used in the manufacture of metal polish
☞	021	A	1/1/95	Abrasive liner for cat litter boxes
☞	007	A	4/2/91	Abrasive wheels (Power operated)
☞	005	A	4/2/91	Abrasives (Dental)
☞	001	A	4/2/91	Absorbing carbons [indicate specific use or industry]
☞	005	A	4/2/91	Acaricides for [indicate specific area of use, e.g., agricultural, commercial, domestic]
☞	015	A	4/2/91	Accordions
☞	016	A	4/2/91	Account books
☞	016	A	4/2/91	Accounting forms
☞	005	A	1/1/95	Acetaminophen [for relief of pain]
☞	017	A	4/2/91	Acetate, for use in [indicate specific field of use] (Semi-processed cellulose)
☞	011	A	4/2/91	Acetylene burners
☞	011	A	4/2/91	Acetylene flares
☞	009	A	4/2/91	Acid hydrometers
☞	029	A	4/2/91	Acidophilus milk
☞	005	A	4/2/91	Acne medications
☞	005	A	4/2/91	Acne treatment preparations
☞	015	A	4/2/91	Acoustic guitars
☞	017	A	4/2/91	Acoustical insulation barrier panels
☞	017	A	4/2/91	Acoustical insulation for buildings
☞	017	A	4/2/91	Acoustical panels for buildings
☞	022	A	4/2/91	Acrylic fibers
☞	017	A	4/2/91	Acrylic molded plastic substances, for use in [indicate specific field of use] (Semi-finished)
☞	017	A	4/2/91	Acrylic resin sheeting for use in the manufacture of laminated glass
☞	001	A	4/2/91	Acrylic resins [indicate specific use or industry](Unprocessed)
☞	017	A	4/2/91	Acrylic sheeting for use in the manufacture of [indicate specific item]
☞	009	A	4/2/91	Actinometers
☞	028	A	4/2/91	Action balls (Rubber)
☞	028	A	4/2/91	Action figures and accessories therefor
☞	028	A	4/2/91	Action figures
☞	028	A	4/2/91	Action skill games
☞	028	A	4/2/91	Action toys (Mechanical)
☞	028	A	4/2/91	Action toys [indicate specific type of operation, e.g., mechanical, electric, etc.]
☞	028	A	4/2/91	Action-type target games
☞	010	A	7/1/94	Acupuncture instruments [electric or non-electric]
☞	010	A	7/1/94	Acupuncture needles
☞	016	A	4/2/91	Adding machine paper
☞	009	A	4/2/91	Adding machines
☞	001	M	3/15/93	Additives (Chemical gasoline)
☞	001	M	3/15/93	Additives (Chemical motor oil)
☞	001	A	4/2/91	Additives (Concrete)
☞	004	A	3/15/93	Additives (Non-chemical gasoline)
☞	004	A	3/15/93	Additives (Non-chemical motor oil)
☞	031	A	4/2/91	Additives for animal feed (Non medicated)
☞	005	A	4/2/91	Additives for livestock feed (Nutritional)
☞	030	A	4/2/91	Additives for non-nutritional purposes (Flavoring)
☞	031	A	4/2/91	Additives for non-nutritional purposes for use as flavoring, ingredient or filler (Animal feed
☞	030	A	4/2/91	Additives for non-nutritional purposes for use as flavoring, ingredient or filler (Food)
☞	001	M	3/15/93	Additives for use in the manufacture of [indicate specific items, e.g., good, pharmaceuticals, c
☞	001	A	4/2/91	Additives to prevent rust (Radiator)
☞	016	A	4/2/91	Address books
☞	016	A	4/2/91	Address labels
☞	016	A	4/2/91	Address plates
☞	016	A	4/2/91	Addressing machines
☞	005	A	7/1/94	Adhesive bandages
☞	017	A	4/2/91	Adhesive bands for sealing cartons for industrial or commercial use
☞	017	A	4/2/91	Adhesive bands for sealing pharmaceutical containers
☞	001	A	4/2/91	Adhesive cement for hobbyists
☞	016	A	4/2/91	Adhesive dispensers for office use (Automatic)
☞	005	A	4/2/91	Adhesive for bandages for skin wounds
☞	017	A	4/2/91	Adhesive packing tape for industrial or commercial use

Trademark Acceptable Identification of Goods and Services Manual

Try to make your description as precise as possible. If your description is too broad, it may describe services in more than one class. And remember, each extra class added to your application will cost another $325. The examiner will probably contact you before adding more classes, so it won't be a surprise. But it may delay the processing of your application.

Date of First Use of Mark Anywhere: The next two sections relating to dates of first use are for use applicants only. ("Intent to use" applicants should skip down to "Final Instructions for All Applicants," below.) Here you are asked to provide the date you first started using the unique part of your domain name—the part to the left of the dot. If you have been using it in an existing business, enter the date you first used that name as part of a commercial transaction. If its first use was as a domain name, then your date of first use is the date your website went live to sell goods or services.

Date of First Use of the Mark in Commerce: Enter the date when you first used the unique part of your domain name in commerce across state, territorial or international borders. If you have an existing business, this date may be different than the date of first use that you just entered. For example, you may have first used the name to market your local business and later gone national or international. The first date would be your use anywhere, and the second date would be the date the scope of your business expanded. If the unique part of your domain name is being used for the first time as your domain name, enter the date of first use.

If you've been using a mark for years and don't remember the exact date of its first use anywhere or across state lines, make your best estimate. Use dated documents that you have gathered over the years, such as old advertisements or business licenses, to help jog your memory. If necessary, use imprecise dates, such as "before March 25, 1998," "on or about January 16, 1975," "in 1966" or "in February 1984." Use the earliest possible date that you can reasonably assert as correct.

Final Instructions for All Applicants

Amount: If you are registering in just one class, as most people do, enter $325. The fee will be $325 more for each additional class.

Payment: Again, check the credit card box if it isn't already checked from your earlier entry.

Declaration: Read it carefully. If there are statements in the declaration that raise serious doubts or questions in your mind, see a trademark lawyer. (For information about how to find a lawyer, see Chapter 9.)

Signature: The information box right above the signature section provides the surprising information that your "signature," when you file online and don't actually sign any paper, can be whatever you choose. You can enter any combination of letters, numbers or other characters as your "signature." Each signature must begin and end with a forward slash (/). For example, /pat smith/; /ps/; and /268-3421/ are all acceptable signatures. There's no trick here. Unless you've developed some special internal system for tracking electronic signatures in your office, entering your own name is the simplest option. Click the signature link just below the information box for the PTO's own words on this subject.

Validate: This process checks your application and alerts you if you forgot to include any information that is mandatory. You will then have a chance to go back and fill in the missing information. A warning message will also appear for non-mandatory missing information, but you are not required to go back and include that information. Once the validation is done, click "Pay/Submit" at the bottom of the Validation screen. Since you are using a credit card for payment, you will next be asked to enter payment information. If your transaction is successful, you will receive a confirmation screen.

Later, you will receive an email acknowledging the submission of your application. Hold on to that email, because it is the only proof you'll have that the PTO has your application. It is also proof of your filing date and contains the serial number assigned to your application.

E. What Happens Next

If you filed a "use" application, you will likely receive some communication from the PTO within three to six months. If there is a problem with your application, you will receive what's called an "action letter." This is simply a letter from your examiner explaining what the problems are. Most problems can be resolved with a phone call to the examiner.

When the examiner approves your application for publication, you will receive a Notice of Publication in the mail. Your mark will then be published in the *Official Gazette* (a PTO journal) for 30 days. During that time, anyone may oppose your registration. Only 3% of all published marks are opposed, so it is very unlikely you will run into trouble.

Once your mark has made it through the 30-day publication period, you will receive a Certificate of Registration. The PTO has lately had a difficult time moving applications through this long process. As a result, it may take a year or more to process your application.

If you filed on an "intent to use" basis, you will need to file an additional document with the PTO when you start using your domain name. This document is called "Statement of Use/Amendment to Allege Use for Intent-to-Use Application." It tells the PTO the date you started using the domain name and completes the registration process. You must also provide a specimen at that time, showing how you are using the domain name.

Down the road, you will need to do a few things to keep your registration in force. For example, between five and six years after the mark is first registered, you'll need to file a document stating that you are still using the mark. And your registration must be renewed every ten years; otherwise it will be automatically cancelled.

The Trademark Registration Kit, by Patricia Gima and Stephen Elias (Nolo), is helpful if you encounter any questions or problems with the trademark examiner during the processing of your trademark application. It also explains how to fill out and file the follow-up document if you file your application on an "intent to use" basis. It also shows you how to maintain your trademark and keep it registered through the years. ■

CHAPTER 9

Help Beyond This Book

We hope this book provides all the information you need to register and protect your domain name. But somewhere along the line, you may need additional help. This chapter covers how to get that help from a lawyer or from your own legal research.

A. Domain Name Disputes

There is really no such thing as a domain name dispute, because each domain name is unique—different from every other domain name. What's known as domain name dispute is always a wrangle between a domain name registrant and the owner of a trademark with which the domain name allegedly conflicts. Throughout this book we have provided guidance on how these types of disputes are likely to be resolved under general trademark principles and the Anti-Cybersquatting Consumer Protection Act of 1999. Additional guidance is sure to come from the administrative procedure recently established by ICANN (described in Chapter 5, Section D2). Under that procedure, each dispute resolution provider's decisions must be posted on the provider's website. Also, most likely, ICANN will aggregate the decisions of all providers and post them in one location on the ICANN website. By browsing these decisions, you will be able to get a real-world feel for what might happen in your particular dispute. You can also consult Sections D and E, below, which discuss how to research trademark law and keep up to date on developments in trademark law and domain names.

B. Trademark Registration Problems

If you file an electronic trademark application (see Chapter 8), you may find you need more help if, for example:

- You filed your trademark application on an "intent to use" basis and now need guidance on the follow-up documents needed to complete your registration or obtain a six-month extension for filing them.
- You filed your trademark application, and the PTO staff has told you there is a problem with it or that they need additional information, or
- You received a certificate of trademark registration for your domain name (congratulations!), but now need guidance on how to maintain your trademark and keep it registered.

For help with these issues, we suggest these resources:

The Trademark Registration Kit, by Patricia Gima and Stephen Elias (Nolo). This book covers all pre- and post-registration issues, including how to manage problems with your application, how to fill out and file follow-up documents for "intent to use" applications and how to maintain your trademark. You can find out more about this book at www.nolo.com.

The *Trademark Manual of Examining Procedure*, the PTO's own manual for evaluating trademark applications, is the bible for trademark examiners, the PTO attorneys who look over your application and ultimately approve or reject your domain name for registration. Virtually every statement they make to you about your application or registration will come with a reference to this publication. You can find this manual at www.uspto.gov. Click Trademark, and then click "Trademark Manual of Examining Procedure."

Federal trademark law, cases and regulations. If you use the *Trademark Manual of Examining Procedure*, you may find it useful to look up sections of the law on which the manual's rules are based. See Section D, below for tips on this process.

C. Other Trademark Issues

If you're looking for information about trademark issues beyond domain names—for example, sorting out trademark disputes or building on your domain name trademark using graphics, packaging, color or product design—then you will want to read *Trademark: Legal Care for Your Business & Product Name,* by Stephen Elias and Kate McGrath (Nolo). It offers comprehensive coverage of trademark law and trademark searching. To find out more about this book, visit www.nolo.com.

UP-TO-DATE INFORMATION ABOUT COURT CASES INVOLVING DOMAIN NAME DISPUTES

Did you read about a recent domain name case in the newspaper, but wanted more information? A website maintained by a law firm (Phillips, Nizer, Benjamin, Krim & Ballon) offers summaries of current cases involving domain name disputes. You will find the website at www.phillipsnizer.com. When you get to the home page, click "Internet Library," and then "Domain Name/Path."

D. Doing Your Own Legal Research

Finding information about the law and ferreting out answers to legal questions is called legal research. If you have a question and can't find the answer in a Nolo book on trademarks or the PTO's website, you may want to do your own legal research.

When it comes to addressing such cutting-edge issues as domain name and trademark conflicts, the Web is the legal research tool of choice. This section gives you an introduction to conducting legal research on the Web. You'll follow these six steps:

1. Find and read the most relevant federal law (statutes).

2. Make sure the law you find is up to date.

3. Find and read relevant regulations issued by the PTO or other agency.

4. Find any court decisions that interpret the relevant statutes and regulations.

5. Read through summaries of the court decisions to find the most relevant case—one that deals with roughly the same facts and issues as your situation.

6. Make sure the court decisions you find are up-to-date.

Legal Research: How to Find and Understand the Law, by Stephen Elias and Susan Levinkind (Nolo), will give you a much more detailed discussion of how to do legal research on the Web and in the law library. It covers the whole process in detail and includes step-by-step instructions for using online research services discussed in this chapter, such as versuslaw.com and keycite.com.

SOME KEY LEGAL TERMS

Statute: A written law passed by Congress or a state legislature and signed into law by the President or a governor. Statutes are often gathered into compilations called "codes," large sets of books that can be found in many public and all law libraries. The federal statutes and the statutes of almost all states are now also available on the Internet.

Case: A term that most often refers to a lawsuit—for example, "I filed my small claims case." However, in our discussion of legal research, "case" refers to a written decision by a trial judge—or, if the trial court's ruling has been appealed, by a panel of appellate judges.

Regulation: A rule that is made by an administrative agency such as the IRS or the PTO. For example, PTO regulations govern the procedures by which trademark applications are filed.

1. Find the Most Relevant and Current Federal Statutes

Because domain names are used across state borders, domain name disputes are usually governed by federal laws. A federal statute that talks about the issue you're interested in is generally the best place to start your research.

Federal trademark laws are collectively known both as the Lanham Act and as the Federal Trademark Act of 1946 (as amended). The Lanham Act is codified (published) in Title 15, Sections 1051 through 1127, of the United States Code. There are two versions of the United States Code on the Web—one maintained by Cornell Law School and the other by the House of Representatives Law Library.

If you know the specific citation of the statute, you will use the House of Representatives Law Library version. For instance, suppose you are looking for the law dealing with trademark dilution, and know that its citation is Title 15, Section 1125 (perhaps you found the citation in some background material you read). You would take these steps:

- Go to www.nolo.com and click the "Online Legal Library" tab at the top of the page. Then click "Statutes." This will take you to the Nolo Legal Research Center.
- Click "Federal Laws."
- Scroll down to the U.S. Code part of the page.
- Enter 15 in the Title box and the section number (for instance 1125) in the section box. Click search.

If you don't have a specific citation, the Cornell site is probably your best bet. For instance, assume that you want to find the federal remedies for trademark infringement. You would take these steps to get to and use the Cornell site:

- Go to www.nolo.com and click the "Online Legal Library" tab at the top of the page. Then click "Statutes." This will take you to the Nolo Legal Research Center.

- Click "Federal Laws."
- Scroll down to the U.S. Code part of the page.
- Click "Browse the U.S. Code at Cornell Law School."
- Click "Title 15" on the home page first if you want to conduct a keyword search of the Lanham Act for "infringement remedies."
- Alternatively, click "Title 15," scroll down the list of chapters until you get to trademarks (Chapter 22), click that link and browse the subject titles. In this example you would find the statute on infringement remedies in Section 1114.

Both sites offer online searching help if you get stuck.

2. Make Sure You're Reading the Latest Version of the Statute

Once you find the statute and section you're looking for, the next step is to make sure the version you're looking at is current. Laws change, and it does you little good to look over a law that is outdated. It takes a lot of time to update the United States Code, and you may be searching a version of the U.S. Code that is really two years out-of-date.

For updating federal statutes, we recommend the Thomas website, at http://thomas.loc.gov. This site provides both pending and recently enacted legislation. Follow the instructions carefully to see whether a particular statute you've found in the code has been amended or even repealed by more recent legislation.

Thomas also helps you research all bills pending before Congress as well as bills recently passed and signed into law by the President. Keeping track of pending bills will give you a leg up on the most recent changes to the U.S. Code should those bills eventually become law. The information on Thomas is organized according to the session of Congress you are searching for—for example, the 106th Congress (1998-1999). If you don't know which period of time you are interested in, you will need to search each session that might be important. Searches in Thomas can be made by topic, by a bill's popular title or by bill number. Finally you can search by public law number—for instance, P.L. 96-4537. The public law number is how a statute is identified until it is placed with other statutes of similar subject matter in the United States Code.

3. Find Relevant Federal Regulations

If you decide to register your domain name as a trademark with the U.S. Patent and Trademark Office (see Chapter 8), you may have occasion to study the trademark rules issued by the PTO. As mentioned, these rules are known as regulations and are published in Title 37, Chapter 1, of the Code of Federal Regulations (C.F.R.). There are two reasons why you would want to look up PTO regulations:

- The PTO refers to a particular regulation when corresponding with you, or on its website.
- You are trying to figure out what a particular statute means and wish to see whether the PTO has interpreted it.

You can find these regulations on the Web by taking the following steps:

- Go to www.nolo.com and click the "Online Legal Library" tab at the top of the page and then click "Statutes." This will take you to the Legal Research Center.
- Click "Federal Laws."
- Scroll down to find the Code of Federal Regulations and enter a keyword or section number. Trademark regulations are found in Title 37, Parts 1-199, Section 2.

4. Find Relevant Court Decisions

If you are trying to answer a legal question, you not only need to know what the underlying laws say, you also need to know what court decisions have had to say on your particular issue. These court decisions are part of what we know as the "common law." As a general rule, the higher the court deciding the case, the more important the case is. The U.S. Supreme Court always has the last word on federal laws.

THE FEDERAL COURT SYSTEM

The federal court system has three tiers. Federal District Courts, the trial courts of the federal system, hear lawsuits for the first time. Certain cases are heard in specialized federal trial courts, such as bankruptcy court or tax court. On the second level are the federal Courts of Appeal, which hear appeals from the District Courts. An appeal is a process by which one party to a lawsuit (usually the losing party) asks a higher court to review the actions of a lower court to correct mistakes or injustice. On the top level is the United States Supreme Court, which hears appeals in a few select cases of its choosing.

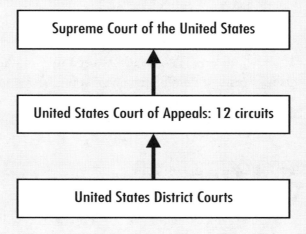

If you have found a relevant statute or regulation, your next best step is to look for court decisions that have interpreted it. The best way to do this is to search for the statute, by number, in a database of court decisions. There are several such databases on the Web. Dollar for dollar, we prefer Versuslaw at www.versuslaw.com. This service costs $6.95 a month and gives you access to most state and federal court decisions. Online help is readily available.

Two sites on the Web do a good job of collecting domain name and trademark cases and providing commentary on what they mean to this rapidly developing legal area:

www.phillipsnizer.com This site, maintained by a New York law firm, offers the best collection of cases dealing with domain name disputes. It provides both a brief and an extensive summary for each case, and a link to the full text of the case if it is available on the Web. When you get to the home page, first click "Internet Library" and then "Domain Name/ Path." The cases are listed in alphabetical order. The more cases you read on this subject, the better feel you'll have for how a court would likely rule in yours if you end up in court.

www.fenwick.com This site is maintained by the renowned intellectual property law firm of Fenwick & West. The Publications page features an excellent scholarly 1998 article by Mitchell Zimmerman and Sally Abel, titled *Securing and Protecting a Domain Name for Your Website*. Although the article itself has not been updated since 1998, it provides a detailed history of domain name disputes and summaries of the major cases that provide the background for today's judicial decisions. The Publications section also offers a newsletter with quarterly updates.

5. Make Sure the Case is Up-to-Date

Once you have found a case that seems to address your question, you will need to check that it is still good law. A case is still "good law" if it hasn't been superseded by a more recent case in a jurisdiction that matters. The best way to do a check on the Web is to use a tool called KeyCite at www.keycite.com. KeyCite costs $3.75 a search (a credit card is required), but it usually takes only one search to find out whether or not the case you found is still good law. KeyCite comes with online help.

E. Finding a Lawyer

If you become involved in a domain name dispute, are having trouble getting your mark registered or simply want some advice from a professional, you may want to consult a lawyer—but not just any lawyer. Start by understanding that if you have read substantial portions of this book you already know more about domain names and trademarks than most lawyers do. This puts you in the difficult position of finding someone who knows more than you do and yet is willing to acknowledge your considerable competence.

We know of no sure-fire way to find such a rare creature, but here are what we think are some good suggestions.

1. Finding a Competent Lawyer

Trademark lawyers (including those who specialize in domain name issues) usually advertise in the Yellow Pages and legal journals as intellectual property specialists, able to handle patent, trademark, copyright and trade secret cases. State and local bar associations may also keep rosters of intellectual property attorneys. Such ads and listings can be misleading because most intellectual property law specialists tend to be very knowledgeable in one or two areas of intellectual property, and only passingly familiar with the others.

You want a lawyer who really knows trademark law as it pertains to domain names, not just someone willing to brush up on the subject at your expense. So when you call on the intellectual property specialist, ask these questions:

- Do you have experience with domain name disputes? If so, what types of disputes have you been involved in? Any experience with domain name litigation (taking a case to court) or NSI or ICANN dispute procedures?
- What percentage of your practice involves domain name disputes?
- How many trademark applications have you filed with the PTO to register domain names?
- Are you a member of the International Trademark Association or the American Intellectual Property Law Association?

The first three questions will help you find a true specialist in this area, while the fourth will help you find a lawyer who is involved enough with trademark issues to join an association of trademark specialists.

2. Finding a Respectful Lawyer

In addition to satisfying yourself that a lawyer is competent, you want to find someone who is reasonably congenial to work with. You don't need us to tell you that many lawyers tend to look down on laypersons when it comes to the lawyer's area of expertise. This means that many of the lawyers you initially encounter are likely to be turned off by your knowledge. Fortunately, however, some lawyers respect their clients' knowledge and know how to work with it rather than against it.

You can find a lawyer who isn't intimidated by a competent client if you:

- explain over the phone that you have been using this book
- articulate exactly what you want the lawyer to do; and

- carefully monitor the lawyer's reaction.

If the lawyer scoffs at the idea of a self-help law book or you get a whiff of, "Don't tell me what you need, I'm the lawyer," go on to the next name on the list. If the response appears to respect your efforts to educate yourself and admits to the possibility that you are a competent human being, make an appointment.

3. Finding an Honest and Conscientious Lawyer

If you are just seeking advice, then you needn't worry much about the lawyer's character. But if you are looking for someone to represent you, the human being you are dealing with becomes paramount. The best analytical trademark lawyer in the world can bring you to financial and emotional ruin, if he or she lacks the ability to understand your needs and to represent you with your best interests in mind.

a. Honesty

A lawyer's financial interest—to run up lots of billable hours over a period of time—is the opposite of yours, which is to arrive at a fast, cost-efficient and reasonably livable resolution of the problem.

Once you understand this, you'll also understand that it is essential that you and your lawyer agree up front about what the lawyer is to do and the amount of control you are to have over the lawyer's activities. Rule One is that the lawyer is working for you, not vice versa. Rule Two is that you have a right to understand the reason for every minute of the lawyer's time that will be billed to you. To make sure you're at least informed about the lawyer's activities and how much you're being charged for them, always ask for a signed agreement between you and your lawyer setting out the lawyer's fees and stating that the lawyer will send you an itemized bill each month. An honest fee agreement will also list all costs that you will be charged for—faxes, photocopies, courier fees and overnight mail fees, for example.

b. Conscientiousness

Your lawyer must be willing to agree to consult you regularly on all phases of the case and to promptly return your phone calls. Although nothing leads to a ruinous relationship faster than bad communication, too few lawyers keep their clients well-posted. Lawyers faced with complaints about their lousy client contact habits often reply that many clients call too often or expect too much. But since the client is paying for the lawyer's time, this seems like a pretty weak excuse.

Your lawyer must also be willing to follow through on your case to its completion. He or she must be ready to stay involved and on top of your case no matter how rocky it gets. For example, if a settlement is expected at the outset, but the case ends up going to court, your lawyer must be willing to go the distance with you and not back out at the last minute. This one is tricky to monitor, because it involves predicting the future. However, as long as good communication is established at the outset, there's an improved chance that your lawyer will give you reliable service. ■

Appendix

International Schedule of Classes of Goods and Services

Goods

1. Chemical products used in industry, science, photography, agriculture, horticulture, forestry; artificial and synthetic resins; plastics in the form of powders, liquids or pastes, for industrial use; manures (natural and artificial); fire extinguishing compositions; tempering substances and chemical preparations for soldering; chemical substances for preserving foodstuffs; tanning substances; adhesive substances used in industry.

2. Paints, varnishes, lacquers; preservatives against rust and against deterioration of wood; colouring matters, dyestuffs; mordants; natural resins; metals in foil and powder form for painters and decorators.

3. Bleaching preparations and other substances for laundry use; cleaning, polishing, scouring and abrasive preparations; soaps; perfumery, essential oils, cosmetics, hair lotions; dentifrices.

4. Industrial oils and greases (other than oils and fats and essential oils); lubricants; dust laying and absorbing compositions; fuels (including motor spirit) and illuminants; candles, tapers, night lights and wicks.

5. Pharmaceutical, veterinary, and sanitary substances; infants' and invalids' foods; plasters, material for bandaging; material for stopping teeth, dental wax, disinfectants; preparations for killing weeds and destroying vermin.

6. Unwrought and partly wrought common metals and their alloys; anchors, anvils, bells, rolled and cast building materials; rails and other metallic materials for railway tracks; chains (except driving chains for vehicles); cables and wires (nonelectric); locksmiths' work; metallic pipes and tubes; safes and cash boxes; steel balls; horseshoes; nails and screws; other goods in nonprecious metal not included in other classes; ores.

7. Machines and machine tools; motors (except for land vehicles); machine couplings and belting (except for land vehicles); large size agricultural implements; incubators.

8. Hand tools and instruments; cutlery, forks and spoons; side arms.

9. Scientific, nautical, surveying and electrical apparatus and instruments (including wireless), photographic, cinematographic, optical, weighing, measuring, signalling, checking (supervision), life-saving and teaching apparatus and instruments; coin or counterfreed apparatus; talking machines; cash registers; calculating machines; fire extinguishing apparatus.

10. Surgical, medical, dental, and veterinary instruments and apparatus (including artificial limbs, eyes and teeth).

11. Installations for lighting, heating, steam generating, cooking, refrigerating, drying, ventilating, water supply, and sanitary purposes.

12. Vehicles; apparatus for locomotion by land, air or water.

13. Firearms; ammunition and projectiles; explosive substances; fireworks.

14. Precious metals and their alloys and goods in precious metals or coated therewith (except cutlery forks and spoons); jewelry, precious stones, horological and other chronometric instruments.

15. Musical instruments (other than talking machines and wireless apparatus).

16. Paper and paper articles, cardboard and cardboard articles; printed matter, newspaper and periodicals, books; bookbinding material; photographs; stationery, adhesive materials (stationery): artists' materials; paint brushes; typewriters and office requisites (other than furniture); instructional and teaching material (other than apparatus); playing cards; printers' type and cliches (stereotype).

17. Gutta percha, india rubber, balata and substitutes, articles made from these substances and not included in other classes; plastics in the form of sheets, blocks and rods, being for use in manufacture; materials for

packing, stopping or insulating; asbestos, mica and their products; hose pipes (nonmetallic).

18. Leather and imitations of leather, and articles made from these materials and not included in other classes; skins, hides; trunks and travelling bags; umbrellas, parasols and walking sticks; whips, harness and saddlery.

19. Building materials, natural and artificial stone, cement, lime, mortar, plaster and gravel; pipes or earthenware or cement; roadmaking materials; asphalt, pitch and bitumen; portable buildings; stone monuments; chimney pots.

20. Furniture, mirrors, picture frames; articles (not included in other classes) of wood, cork, reeds, cane, wicker, horn, bone, ivory, whalebone, shell, amber, mother-of-pearl, meerschaum, celluloid, substitutes for all these materials, or of plastics.

21. Small domestic utensils and containers (not of precious metals, or coated therewith); combs and sponges; brushes (other than paint brushes); brushmaking materials; instruments and material for cleaning purposes, steel wool; unworked or semi-worked glass (excluding glass used in building); glassware, porcelain and earthenware, not included in other classes.

22. Ropes, string, nets, tents, awnings, tarpaulins, sails, sacks; padding and stuffing materials (hair, kapok, feathers, seaweed, etc.); raw fibrous textile materials.

23. Yarns, threads.

24. Tissues (piece goods); bed and table covers; textile articles not included in other classes.

25. Clothing, including boots, shoes and slippers.

26. Lace and embroidery, ribbons and braid; buttons, press buttons, hooks and eyes, pins and needles; artificial flowers.

27. Carpets, rugs, mats and matting; linoleums and other materials for covering existing floors; wall hangings (nontextile).

28. Games and playthings; gymnastic and sporting articles (except clothing); ornaments and decorations for Christmas trees.

29. Meats, fish, poultry and game; meat extracts; preserved, dried and cooked fruits and vegetables; jellies, jams; eggs, milk and other dairy products; edible oils and fats; preserves, pickles.

30. Coffee, tea, cocoa, sugar, rice, tapioca, sago, coffee substitutes; flour, and preparations made from cereals; bread, biscuits, cakes, pastry and confectionery, ices; honey, treacle; yeast, baking powder; salt, mustard, pepper, vinegar, sauces, spices; ice.

31. Agricultural, horticultural and forestry products and grains not included in other classes; living animals; fresh fruits and vegetables; seeds; live plants and flowers; foodstuffs for animals, malt.

32. Beer, ale and porter; mineral and aerated waters and other nonalcoholic drinks; syrups and other preparations for making beverages.

33. Wines, spirits and liqueurs.

34. Tobacco, raw or manufactured; smokers' articles; machines.

Services

35. Advertising and business.

36. Insurance and financial.

37. Construction and repair.

38. Communication.

39. Transportation and Storage.

40. Material treatment.

41. Education and entertainment.

42. Miscellaneous.

Descriptions of Goods and Services (From USTA—International Classes)*

Goods

Class I: Chemicals

Chemicals used in industry, science and photography as well as in agriculture, horticulture and forestry; unprocessed artificial resins, unprocessed plastics; manures; fire extinguishing compositions; tempering and soldering preparations; chemical substances for preserving foodstuffs; tanning substances; adhesives used in industry.

This class includes mainly chemical products used in industry, science and agriculture, including those which go to the making of products belonging to other classes.

Includes, in particular: compost; salt for preserving other than for foodstuffs.

Does not include, in particular: chemical products for use in medical science (Cl. 5); fungicides, herbicides and preparations for destroying vermin (Cl. 5); raw natural resins (Cl. 2); salt for preserving foodstuffs (Cl. 30); adhesives for stationery purposes (Cl. 16); straw mulch (Cl. 31).

Class 2: Paints

Paints, varnishes, lacquers; preservatives against rust and against deterioration of wood; colourants; mordants; raw natural resins; metals in foil and powder form for painters, decorators, printers and artists.

This class includes mainly paints, colourants and preparations used for the protection against corrosion.

---

* Adapted from *The Trademark Manual of Examining Procedure,* published by the U.S. Trademark and Patent Office.

Includes, in particular: paints, varnishes and lacquers for industry, handicrafts and arts; dyestuffs for clothing; colourants for foodstuffs and beverages.

Does not include, in particular: laundry blueing (Cl. 3); cosmetic dyes (Cl. 3); insulating paints and varnishes (Cl. 17); paint boxes (articles for use in school) (Cl. 16); unprocessed artificial resins (Cl. 1); mordants for seed (Cl. 5).

Class 3: Cosmetics and cleaning preparations

Bleaching preparations and other substances for laundry use; cleaning, polishing, scouring and abrasive preparations; soaps; perfumery, essential oils, cosmetics, hair lotions; dentifrices.

This class includes mainly cleaning preparations and toilet preparations.

Includes, in particular: deodorants for personal use; sanitary preparations being toiletries.

Does not include, in particular: chemical chimney cleaners (Cl. 1); degreasing preparations for use in manufacturing processes (Cl. 1); sharpening stones and grindstones (handtools) (Cl. 8); deodorants other than for personal use (Cl. 5).

Class 4: Lubricants and fuels

Industrial oils and greases; lubricants; dust absorbing, wetting and binding compositions; fuels (including motor spirit) and illuminants; candles, wicks.

This class includes mainly industrial oils and greases, fuels and illuminants.

Does not include, in particular: certain special industrial oils and greases (consult the Alphabetical List of Goods).

Class 5: Pharmaceuticals

Pharmaceutical, veterinary and sanitary preparations; dietetic substances adapted for medical use, food for babies; plasters, materials for dressings; material for stopping teeth, dental wax; disinfectants; preparations for destroying vermin; fungicides, herbicides.

This class includes mainly pharmaceuticals and other preparations for medical purposes.

Includes, in particular: sanitary preparations for medical purposes and for personal hygiene; deodorants other than for personal use; cigarettes without tobacco, for medical purposes.

Does not include, in particular: sanitary preparations being toiletries (Cl. 3); deodorants for personal use (Cl. 3); supportive bandages (Cl. 10).

Class 6: Metal goods

Common metals and their alloys; metal building materials; transportable buildings of metal; materials of metal for railway tracks; non-electric cables and wires of common metal; ironmongery, small items of metal hardware; pipes and tubes of metal; safes; goods of common metal not included in other classes; ores.

This class includes mainly unwrought and partly wrought common metals as well as simple products made of them.

Does not include, in particular: mercury, antimony, alkaline and alkaline-earth metals (Cl. 1); metals in foil and powder form for painters, decorators, printers and artists (Cl. 2); bauxite (Cl. 1).

Class 7: Machinery

Machines and machine tools; motors (except for land vehicles); machine coupling and belting (except for land vehicles); agricultural implements; incubators for eggs.

This class includes mainly machines, machine tools, engines and motors.

Does not include, in particular: certain special machines and machine tools (consult the Alphabetical List of Goods); motors for land vehicles and their parts (Cl. 12); hand tools and implements, hand operated (Cl. 8).

Class 8: Hand tools

Hand tools and implements (hand operated); cutlery, forks and spoons; side arms; razors.

This class includes mainly hand operated implements used as tools in the respective professions.

Includes, in particular: cutlery of precious metals; electric razors and clippers (hand instruments).

Does not include, in particular: certain special instruments (consult the Alphabetical List of Goods); machine tools and implements driven by a motor (Cl. 7); surgical cutlery (Cl. 10); paper-knives (Cl. 16); fencing weapons (Cl. 28).

Class 9: Electrical and scientific apparatus

Scientific, nautical, surveying, electric, photographic, cinematographic, optical, weighing, measuring, signalling, checking (supervision), life-saving and teaching apparatus and instruments; apparatus for recording, transmission or reproduction of sound or images; magnetic data carriers, recording discs; automatic vending machines and mechanisms for coin-operated apparatus; cash registers, calculating machines and data processing equipment; fire-extinguishing apparatus.

Includes, in particular: apparatus and instruments for scientific research in laboratories; apparatus and instruments for controlling ships, such as apparatus and instruments, for measuring and for transmitting orders; the following electrical apparatus and instruments:

    a. certain electrothermic tools and apparatus, such as electric soldering irons, electric flat irons which, if they were not electric, would belong to Class 8;

    b. apparatus and devices which, if not electrical, would be listed in various classes, i.e., electrically heated cushions (not for medical purposes), electric kettles, electrically heated clothing and other articles worn on the body, cigar-lighters for automobiles;

c. electrical apparatus for the household, used for cleaning (electric suction-cleaners and floor polishers for domestic use) which, if not electrical, would belong to Class 21;

protractors; punched card office machines; amusement apparatus adapted for use with television receivers only.

Does not include, in particular: the following electrical apparatus and instruments:

a. electromechanical apparatus for the kitchen (grinders and mixers for foodstuffs, fruitpresses, electrical coffee mills, etc.), and certain other apparatus and instruments driven by an electrical motor, all coming under Class 7;

b. electric razors and clippers (hand instruments) (Cl. 8); electric toothbrushes and combs (Cl. 21);

c. electrically heated blankets (Cl. 10); electrical apparatus for space heating or for the heating of liquids, for cooking, ventilating, etc. (Cl. 11);

clocks and watches and other chronometric instruments (Cl. 14); control clocks (Cl. 14).

Class 10: Medical apparatus

Surgical, medical, dental and veterinary apparatus and instruments, artificial limbs, eyes and teeth; orthopedic articles; suture materials.

This class includes mainly medical apparatus, instruments and articles.

Includes, in particular: special furniture for medical use; hygienic rubber articles (consult the Alphabetical List of Goods); supportive bandages.

Class 11: Environmental control apparatus

Apparatus for lighting, heating, steam generating, cooking, refrigerating, drying, ventilating, water supply and sanitary purposes.

Includes, in particular: air conditioning apparatus; electric foot-warmers; electric cooking utensils.

Does not include, in particular: steam producing apparatus (parts of machines) (Cl. 7); electric kettles (Cl. 9).

Class 12: Vehicles

Vehicles; apparatus for locomotion by land, air or water.

Includes, in particular: engines for land vehicles; transmission couplings and belting for land vehicles; air cushion vehicles.

Does not include, in particular: certain parts of vehicles (consult the Alphabetical List of Goods); railway material of metal (Cl. 6); engines, transmission couplings and belting other than for land vehicles (Cl. 7).

Class 13: Firearms

Firearms; ammunition and projectiles; explosives; fireworks.

This class includes mainly firearms and pyrotechnical products.

Does not include, in particular: matches (Cl. 34).

Class 14: Jewelry

Precious metals and their alloys and goods in precious metals or coated therewith, not included in other classes; jewelry, precious stones; horological and chronometric instruments.

This class includes mainly precious metals, goods in precious metals and, in general jewelry, clocks and watches.

Includes, in particular: jewelry (i.e., imitation jewelry and jewelry of precious metal and stones); cuff links, tie pins; objects of art fashioned in bronze.

Does not include, in particular: certain goods in precious metals (classified according to their function or purpose), for example: metals in foil and powder form for painters, decorators, printers and artists (Cl. 2); amalgam of gold for dentists (Cl. 5); cutlery (Cl. 8); electric contacts (Cl. 9); writing pens of gold (Cl. 16); objects of art not in precious metal nor in bronze are classified according to the material of which they consist.

Class 15: Musical instruments

Musical instruments.

Includes, in particular: mechanical pianos and their accessories; musical boxes; electrical and electronical musical instruments.

Does not include, in particular: apparatus for the recording, transmission, amplification and reproduction of sound (Cl. 9).

Class 16: Paper goods and printed matter

Paper, cardboard and goods made from these materials, not included in other classes; printed matter; bookbinding material, photographs; stationery; adhesives for stationery or household purposes; artists' materials; paint brushes; typewriters and office requisites (except furniture); instructional and teaching material (except apparatus); plastic materials for packaging (not included in other classes); playing cards; printers' type; printing blocks.

This class includes mainly paper, goods made from that material and office requisites.

Includes, in particular: paper-knives; duplicators; plastic sheets, sacks and bags for wrapping and packaging.

Does not include, in particular: certain goods made of paper and cardboard (consult the Alphabetical List of Goods); colours (Cl. 2); hand tools for artists (for example: spatulas, sculptors' chisels) (Cl. 8).

Class 17: Rubber goods

Rubber, gutta-percha, gum, asbestos, mica and goods made from these materials and not included in other classes; plastics in extruded form for use in manufacture; packing, stopping and insulating materials; flexible pipes, not of metal.

This class includes mainly electrical, thermal and acoustic insulating materials and plastics, being for use in manufacture in the form of sheets, blocks and rods.

Includes, in particular: rubber material for recapping tyres; padding and stuffing materials of rubber or plastics; floating anti-pollution barriers.

Class 18: Leather goods

Leather and imitations of leather, and goods made of these materials and not included in other classes; animal skins, hides; trunks and travelling bags; umbrellas, parasols and walking sticks; whips; harness and saddlery.

This class includes mainly leather, leather imitations, travel goods not included in other classes and saddlery.

Does not include, in particular: clothing, footwear, headgear (consult the Alphabetical List of Goods).

Class 19: Non-metallic building materials

Building materials (non-metallic); non-metallic rigid pipes for building; asphalt, pitch and bitumen; non-metallic transportable buildings; monuments, not of metal.

This class includes mainly non-metallic building materials.

Includes, in particular: semi-worked woods (for example: beams, planks, panels); veneers; building glass (for example: floor slabs, glass tiles); glass granules for marking out roads; letter boxes of masonry.

Does not include, in particular: cement preservatives and cement-waterproofing preparations (Cl. 1); fireproofing preparations (Cl. 1).

Class 20: Furniture and articles not otherwise classified

Furniture, mirrors, picture frames; goods (not included in other classes) of wood, cork, reed, cane, wicker, horn, bone, ivory, whalebone, shell, amber, mother-of-pearl, meerschaum and substitutes for all these materials, or of plastics.

This class includes mainly furniture and its parts and plastic goods, not included in other classes.

Includes, in particular: metal furniture and furniture for camping; bedding (for example: mattresses, spring mattresses, pillows); looking glasses and furnishing or toilet mirrors; registration number plates not of metal; letter boxes not of metal or masonry.

Does not include, in particular: certain special types of mirrors, classified according to their function or purpose (consult the Alphabetical List of Goods); special furniture for laboratories (Cl. 9); special furniture for medical use (Cl. 10); bedding linen (Cl. 24); eiderdowns (Cl. 24).

Class 21: Housewares and glass

Household or kitchen utensils and containers (not of precious metal or coated therewith); combs and sponges; brushes (except paint brushes); brush-making materials; articles for cleaning purposes; steel wool; unworked or semi-worked glass (except glass used in building); glassware, porcelain and earthenware not included in other classes.

This class includes mainly small, hand-operated, utensils and apparatus for household and kitchen use as well as toilet utensils, glassware and articles in porcelain.

Includes, in particular: utensils and containers for household and kitchen use, for example: kitchen utensils, pails, and pans of iron, aluminum, plastics and other materials, small hand-operated apparatus for mincing, grinding, pressing, etc.; candle extinguishers, not of precious metal; electric combs; electric toothbrushes; dish stands and decanter stands.

Does not include, in particular: small apparatus for mincing, grinding, pressing, etc., driven by electricity (Cl. 7); cooking utensils, electric (Cl. 11); razors and shaving apparatus, clippers (hand instruments), metal implements and utensils for manicure and pedicure (Cl. 8); cleaning preparations, soaps, etc. (Cl. 3); certain goods made of glass, porcelain and earthenware (consult the Alphabetical List of Goods); toilet mirrors (Cl. 20).

Class 22: Cordage and fibers

Ropes, string, nets, tents, awnings, tarpaulins, sails, sacks and bags (not included in other classes); padding and stuffing materials (except of rubber or plastics); raw fibrous textile materials.

This class includes mainly rope and sail manufacture products, padding and stuffing materials and raw fibrous textile materials.

Includes, in particular: cords and twines in natural or artificial textile fibres, paper or plastics.

Does not include, in particular: strings for musical instruments (Cl. 15); certain nets, sacs and bags (consult the Alphabetical List of Goods).

Class 23: Yarns and threads

Yarns and threads, for textile use.

Class 24: Fabrics

Textiles and textile goods, not included in other classes; bed and table covers.

This class includes mainly textiles (piece goods) and textile covers for household use.

Includes, in particular: bedding linen of paper.

Does not include, in particular: certain special textiles (consult the Alphabetical List of Goods); electrically heated blankets (Cl. 10); table linen of paper (Cl. 16); horse blankets (Cl. 18).

Class 25: Clothing

Clothing, footwear, headgear.

Does not include, in particular: certain clothing and footwear for special use (consult the Alphabetical List of Goods).

Class 26: Fancy goods

Lace and embroidery, ribbons and braid; buttons, hooks and eyes, pins and needles; artificial flowers.

This class includes mainly dressmakers' articles.

Includes, in particular: slide fasteners.

Does not include, in particular: certain special types of hooks (consult the Alphabetical List of Goods); certain special types of needles (consult the Alphabetical List of Goods); yarns and threads for textile use (Cl. 23).

Class 27: Floor coverings

Carpets, rugs, mats and matting, linoleum and other materials for covering existing floors; wall hangings (non-textile).

This class includes mainly products intended to be added as furnishings to previously constructed floors and walls.

Class 28: Toys and sporting goods

Games and playthings; gymnastic and sporting articles not included in other classes; decorations for Christmas trees.

Includes, in particular: fishing tackle; equipment for various sports and games.

Does not include, in particular: playing cards (Cl. 16); diving equipment (Cl. 9); clothing for gymnastics and sports (Cl. 25); fishing nets (Cl. 22); Christmas tree candles (Cl. 4); electrical lamps (garlands) for Christmas trees (Cl. 11); confectionery and chocolate decorations for Christmas trees (Cl. 30); amusement apparatus adapted for use with television receivers only (Cl. 9).

Class 29: Meat and processed foods

Meat, fish, poultry and game; meat extracts; preserved, dried and cooked fruits and vegetables; jellies, jams; eggs, milk and milk products; edible oils and fats; salad dressings; preserves.

This class includes mainly foodstuffs of animal origin as well as vegetables and other horticultural comestible products which are prepared for consumption or conservation.

Includes, in particular: mollusca and crustacea (living as well as not living); milk beverages (milk predominating).

Does not include, in particular: living animals (Cl. 31); certain foodstuffs of plant origin (consult the Alphabetical List of Goods); baby food (Cl. 5); dietetic substances adapted for medical use (Cl. 5); fertilized eggs for hatching (Cl. 31); foodstuffs for animals (Cl. 31).

Class 30: Staple foods

Coffee, tea, cocoa, sugar, rice, tapioca, sago, artificial coffee; flour and preparations made from cereals, bread, pastry and confectionery, ices; honey, treacle; yeast, baking-powder; salt, mustard; vinegar, sauces (except salad dressings); spices; ice.

This class includes mainly foodstuffs of plant origin prepared for consumption or conservation as well as auxiliaries intended for the improvement of the flavour of food.

Includes, in particular: beverages with coffee, cocoa or chocolate base, cereals prepared for human consumption (for example: oat flakes and those made of other cereals).

Does not include, in particular: certain foodstuffs of plant origin (consult the Alphabetical List of Goods); salt for preserving other than for foodstuffs (Cl. 1); medicinal teas and dietetic substances adapted for medical use (Cl. 5); baby food (Cl. 5); raw cereals (Cl. 31); foodstuffs for animals (Cl. 31).

Class 31: Natural agricultural products

Agricultural, horticultural and forestry products and grains not included in other classes; living animals; fresh fruits and vegetables; seeds, natural plants and flowers; foodstuffs for animals, malt.

This class includes mainly land products not having been subjected to any form of preparation for consumption, living animals and plants as well as foodstuffs for animals.

Includes, in particular: raw woods; raw cereals; fertilized eggs for hatching.

Does not include, in particular: semi-worked woods (Cl. 19); rice (Cl. 30); tobacco (Cl. 34); cultures of micro-organisms and leeches for medical purposes (Cl. 5); fishing bait (Cl. 28); mollusca and crustacea (living as well as not living) (Cl. 29).

Class 32: Light beverages

Beers; mineral and aerated waters and other non-alcoholic drinks; fruit drinks and fruit juices; syrups and other preparations for making beverages.

This class includes mainly non-alcoholic beverages, as well as beer.

Includes, in particular: de-alcoholised drinks.

Does not include, in particular: beverages for medical purposes (Cl. 5); milk beverages (milk predominating) (Cl. 29); beverages with coffee, cocoa or chocolate base (Cl. 30).

Class 33: Wine and spirits

Alcoholic beverages (except beers).

Does not include, in particular: medicinal drinks (Cl. 5); de-alcoholised drinks (Cl. 32).

Class 34: Smokers' articles

Tobacco; smokers' articles; matches.

Includes, in particular: tobacco substitutes (not for medical purposes).

Does not include, in particular: certain smokers' articles in precious metal (Cl. 14) (consult the Alphabetical List of Goods); cigarettes without tobacco, for medical purposes (Cl.5).

Class 35: Advertising and business

This class includes mainly services rendered by persons or organizations principally with the object of:

1. help in the working or management of a commercial undertaking, or
2. help in the management of the business affairs or commercial functions of an industrial or commercial enterprise, as well as services rendered by advertising establishments primarily undertaking communications to the public, declarations or announcements by all means of diffusion and concerning all kinds of goods or services.

Includes, in particular: services consisting of the registration, transcription, composition, compilation, transmission or systematization of written communications and registrations, and also the exploitation or compilation of mathematical or statistical data; services of advertising agencies and services such as the distribution of prospectuses, directly or through the post, or the distribution of samples. This class may refer to advertising in connection with other services, such as those concerning bank loans or advertising by radio.

Does not include, in particular: activity of an enterprise the primary function of which is the sale of goods, i.e., of a so-called commercial enterprise; services such as evaluations and reports of engineers which do not directly refer to the working or management of affairs in a commercial or industrial enterprise (consult the Alphabetical List of Services); professional consultations and the drawing up of plans not connected with the conduct of business (Cl. 42).

Class 36: Insurance and financial

This class includes mainly services rendered in financial and monetary affairs and services rendered in relation to insurance contracts of all kinds.

Includes, in particular: services relating to financial or monetary affairs comprise the following:

a. services of all the banking establishments, or institutions connected with them such as exchange brokers or clearing services;

b. services of credit institutions other than banks such as co-operative credit associations, individual financial companies, lenders, etc.;

c. services of "investment trusts," of holding companies;

d. services of brokers dealing in shares and property;

e. services connected with monetary affairs vouched for by trustees;

f. services rendered in connection with the issue of travelers' cheques and letters of credit; services of realty administrators of buildings, i.e., services of letting or valuation, or financing; services dealing with insurance such as services rendered by agents or brokers engaged in insurance, services rendered to insurers and insured, and insurance underwriting services.

Class 37: Construction and repair

This class includes mainly services rendered by contractors or subcontractors in the construction or making of permanent buildings, as well as services rendered by persons or organisations engaged in the restoration of objects to their original condition or in their preservation without altering their physical or chemical properties.

Includes, in particular: services relating to the construction of buildings, roads, bridges, dams or transmission lines and services of undertakings specializing in the field of construction such as those of painters, plumbers, heating installers or roofers; services auxiliary to construction services like inspections of construction plans; services consisting of hiring of tools or building materials; repair services, i.e. services which undertake to put any object into good condition after wear, damage, deterioration or partial destruction (restoration of an existing building or another object that has become imperfect and is to be restored to its original condition); various repair services such as those in the fields of electricity, furniture, instruments, tools, etc.; services of maintenance for preserving an object in its original condition without changing any of its properties (for the difference between this class and Class 40 see the explanatory note of Class 40).

Does not include, in particular: services consisting of storage of goods such as clothes or vehicles (Cl. 39); services connected with dyeing of cloth or clothes (Cl. 40).

Class 38: Communication

This class includes mainly services allowing at least one person to communicate with another by a sensory means. Such services include those which:

1. allow a person to talk to another,
2. transmit messages from one person to another, and
3. place a person in oral or visual communication with another (radio and television).

Includes, in particular: services which consist essentially of the diffusion of radio or television programmes.

Does not include, in particular: radio advertising services (Cl. 35).

Class 39: Transportation and storage

This class includes mainly services rendered in transporting people or goods from one place to another (by rail, road, water, air or pipeline) and services necessarily connected with such transport, as well as services relating to the storing of goods in a warehouse or other building for their preservation or guarding.

Includes, in particular: services rendered by companies exploiting stations, bridges, railroad ferries, etc., used by the transporter; services connected with the hiring of transport vehicles; services connected with maritime tugs, unloading, the functioning of ports and docks and the salvaging of wrecked ships and their cargoes; services connected with the functioning of airports; services connected with the packaging and parcelling of goods before dispatch; services consisting of information about journeys or the transport of goods by brokers and tourist agencies, information relating to tariffs, timetables and methods of transport; services relating to the inspection of vehicles or goods before transport.

Does not include, in particular: services relating to advertising transport undertakings such as the distribution of prospectuses or advertising on the radio (Cl. 35); services relating to the issuing of travelers' cheques or letters of credit by brokers or travel agents (Cl. 36); services relating to insurances (commercial, fire or life) during the transport of persons or goods (Cl. 36); services rendered by the maintenance and repair of vehicles, nor the maintenance or repair of objects connected with the transport of persons or goods (Cl. 37); services relating to reservation of rooms in a hotel by travel agents or brokers (Cl. 42).

Class 40: Material treatment

This class includes mainly services not included in other classes, rendered by the mechanical or chemical processing or transformation of objects or inorganic or organic substances.

For the purposes of classification, the mark is considered a service mark only in cases where processing or transformation is effected for the account of another person. A mark is considered a trademark in all cases where the substance or object is marketed by the person who processed or transformed it.

Includes, in particular: services relating to transformation of an object or substance and any process involving a change in its essential properties (for example, dyeing a garment); consequently, a maintenance service, although usually in Class 37, is included in Class 40 if it entails such a change (for example, the chroming of motor vehicle bumpers);

services of material treatment which may be present during production of any substance or object other than a building; for example, services which involve shaping, polishing by abrasion or metal coating.

Does not include, in particular: repair services (Cl. 37).

Class 41: Education and entertainment

This class contains mainly services rendered by persons or institutions in the development of the mental faculties of persons or animals, as well as services intended to entertain or to engage the attention.

Includes, in particular: services consisting of all forms of education of persons or training of animals; services having the basic aim of the entertainment, amusement or recreation of people.

Class 42: Miscellaneous

This class contains all services which could not be placed in other classes.

Includes, in particular: services rendered in procuring lodgings, rooms and meals, by hotels, boarding houses, tourist camps, tourist houses, dude ranches, sanatoria, rest homes and convalescence homes; services rendered by establishments essentially engaged in procuring food or drink prepared for consumption; such services can be rendered by restaurants, self-service restaurants, canteens, etc.; personal services rendered by establishments to meet individual needs; such services may include social escorts, beauty salons, hairdressing salons, funeral establishments or crematoria; services rendered by persons, individually or collectively, as a member of an organisation, requiring a high degree of mental activity and relating to theoretical or practical aspects of complex branches of human effort; the services rendered by these persons demand of them a deep and extensive university education or equivalent experience; such services rendered by representatives of professions such as engineers, chemists, physicists, etc., are included in this class; services of travel agents or brokers ensuring hotel accommodation for travelers;

services of engineers engaged in valuing, estimates, research and reports; services (not included in other classes) rendered by associations to their own members.

Does not include, in particular: professional services giving direct aid in the operations or functions of a commercial undertaking (Cl. 35); services for travelers rendered by travel agencies (Cl. 39); performances of singers or dancers in orchestras or operas (Cl. 41).

1401.02(b)   Short Titles for International Trademark Classes [R-6]

The United States Patent and Trademark Office associates the following word titles with the respective international trademark class numbers:

Goods

1. Chemicals
2. Paints
3. Cosmetics and cleaning preparations
4. Lubricants and fuels
5. Pharmaceuticals
6. Metal goods
7. Machinery
8. Hand tools
9. Electrical and scientific apparatus
10. Medical apparatus
11. Environmental control apparatus
12. Vehicles
13. Firearms
14. Jewelry
15. Musical instruments
16. Paper goods and printed matter

17. Rubber goods

18. Leather goods

19. Non-metallic building materials

20. Furniture and articles not otherwise classified

21. Housewares and glass

22. Cordage and fibers

23. Yarns and threads

24. Fabrics

25. Clothing

26. Fancy goods

27. Floor coverings

28. Toys and sporting goods

29. Meats and processed foods

30. Staple foods

31. Natural agricultural products

32. Light beverages

33. Wine and spirits

34. Smokers' articles

Services

35. Advertising and business

36. Insurance and financial

37. Construction and repair

38. Communication

39. Transportation and storage

40. Material treatment

41. Education and entertainment

42. Miscellaneous

These short titles are not an official part of the international classification. Their purpose is to provide a means by which the general content of numbered international classes can be quickly identified. Therefore the titles selected consist of short terms which generally correspond to the major content of each class but which are not intended to be more than merely suggestive of the content. Because of their nature these titles will not necessarily disclose the classification of specific items. The titles are not designed to be used for classification but only as information to assist in the identification of numbered classes. For determining classification of particular goods and services and for full disclosure of the contents of international classes, it is necessary to refer to the Alphabetical List of Goods and Services and to the names of international classes and the Explanatory Notes in the volume entitled "International Classification of Goods and Services for the Purposes of the Registration of Marks" (4th ed. 1983), published by the World Intellectual Property Organization (WIPO). The full names of international classes appear in Section 6.1 of the Trademark Rules of Practice. 37 CFR § 6.1.

The short titles are printed in the OFFICIAL GAZETTE in association with the international class numbers under MARKS PUBLISHED FOR OPPOSITION, Sections 1 and 2, under TRADEMARK REGISTRATIONS ISSUED, PRINCIPAL REGISTER, Section 1, and under SUPPLEMENTAL REGISTER, Sections 1 and 2.

The international trademark classification was adopted by the United States as its system of classification as of September 1, 1973 (see TMEP section 1401.02 and 911 O.G. TM 210, June 26, 1973).

The use of short titles was announced in the *Official Gazette* of July 16, 1974 (924 O.G. TM 155).

1401.03   Marking Classification on Copies in Search Library (R-5]

Beginning September 1, 1973, all published marks, registrations and renewals will be assigned not only an international class number but also a class number according to prior United States classification.

By placing a prior United States class number, as well as an international class number, on copies of registrations which are placed in the Trademark Search Library after the international classification becomes official, searching may continue to be conducted on the basis of the prior United States classification. Registration copies placed in the Search Library prior to September 1, 1973, bear prior United States class numbers, so that placing prior United States class numbers on registration copies on and after September 1, 1973, will provide continuity in the identification of classes on copies of registrations.

Identification and Classification of Certain Computer Related Goods and Services

Class 9:

Pre-recorded software on CD-ROMs, diskettes, magnetic tapes, etc. is in Class 9. The description must provide an indication of the subject matter or function of the software and the subject matter or function indication must be detailed and specific. Very broad statements of function such as "computer programs for business use" are not acceptable.

Class 9:

Computer software [specify the function of the programs, e.g., for use in data base management, for use as a spreadsheet, for word processing, etc.] that is downloaded from a remote computer site" is classified in Class 9.

NOTE: This is a change in classification policy. Previously, "downloadable computer software" was being classified in International Class 42. After a review of this policy, the PTO has decided to classify downloadable software in Class 9 with other software. The placement of downloadable software in International Class 9 is consistent with the practice in a number of other countries.

Class 16:

Only hard copy publications, e.g., printed magazines and books, are considered to be Class 16 goods.

NOTE: Magazines or books that are downloadable from a computer network are not considered to be "hard goods" and they are classified in International Class 42, rather than Class 16. The service is defined as providing the publications on a global computer network and the subject matter of the publications must be specified. If an entire magazine or other publication is presented at the web site, the computer service of providing that publication electronically is considered to be the primary service involved in this activity. The service being provided is that of making available magazines, books and/or other publications via a computer. Appropriate language for these services would be: "Computer services, namely, providing on-line [indicate specific nature of the publication] in the field of [indicate subject matter of the publication]" in Class 42. As with Class 16 publications, the subject matter of the publication does not affect the classification of this service.

Classes 35, 36, 37, 39, 40 & 41:

Any activity consisting of a service that ordinarily falls in these classes (e.g. computer games, various financial transactions, etc.) that also happens to be provided by means of a global computer network, is classified in the class where the underlying service is classified. For example, banking services are in Class 36 whether provided in a bank or on-line by means of global computer network. Similarly, the service of providing information by means of a global computer network is classified in the class of the information subject. Entities who offer these services by computer are considered "content providers," that is, they provide the information or substantive content for a web site and/or home page. A recitation of services for these specific content providers should read "providing information in the field of…by means of a global computer network." The service would be classified by the class of the subject matter of the information. If an entity provides information in a wide variety of fields, this must be reflected in the identification and the service may be classified in Class 42 (e.g., providing information in a wide variety of fields by means of a global computer information network.) Please note that the term "access" should be reserved for use in recitations for network service providers, such as, America OnLine®, Prodigy® and CompuServe®. The PTO considers the use of the term "access" by a content provider to be inaccurate because it causes confusion with the service provider activities.

These guidelines also apply to activities in Classes 38 and 42, however, the comments below also apply to Classes 38 and 42.

Class 38:

The service of providing telecommunications connections to a global computer network is classified in Class 38. These services are purely telecommunications "connections" such as those provided by AT&T®, MCI® or other telecommunications providers. It is ONLY the technical means by which one computer can communicate with another. The telecommunications provider does NOT provide the computer hardware that stores and processes the date: it provides the means by which data is transferred. This service connects the user to the "link provider" (see Class 42 discussion below) or the web site itself.

Class 42:

The service of providing multiple-user access to a global computer information network for the transfer and dissemination of a wide range of information is classified in International Class 42. This language covers those services provided by entities such as America OnLine®, Prodigy® and CompuServe®. They provide the computer service (often using the telecommunications services of other entities as described above in Class 38) that enable computer users to access data bases and home pages of others. These entities are considered "link providers" in that they provide the computer/server connection required for computer users to access a content provider. The word "access" should be limited to these services and should not be used in describing the service of a content provider.

NOTE: A single entity may provide one or more of the services described above. However, each service must be properly identified and classified.

General Comment:

The term "Internet" is still the subject of a proceeding at the Trademark Trial and Appeal Board. Therefore, this term should not be used in identifying any goods or services connected with a global computer information network. Language such as "global computer information network" or a substantive equivalent should be used instead of the term "Internet." ∎

INDEX

■

more from

nolo.com
LAW FOR ALL

TRADEMARK
Legal Care for Your Business & Product Name
by Attorneys Stephen Elias and Kate McGrath

Trademarks — the names and symbols that identify your business, brand and products in the marketplace — are important assets that you need to choose carefully and protect. With *Trademark*, you get the most up-to-date information you need to defend your creations. Includes all necessary forms and instructions to register a trademark or service mark with the U.S. Patent & Trademark Office.

$34.95/TRD

THE COPYRIGHT HANDBOOK
How to Protect and Use Written Works
4th Edition

By Attorney Stephen Fishman

This must-have handbook provides you with every necessary form to protect written expression under U.S. and international copyright law. It discusses the Digital Millennium Copyright Act, new fees and registration forms, the 20-year extension of copyright terms, Tasini v. New York Times and the resulting decision that affects all freelance writers, and more. All 23 forms come as tear-outs and on CD-ROM.

$34.95/COHA

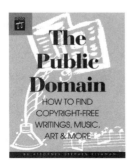

THE PUBLIC DOMAIN
How to Find Copyright-Free Writings, Music, Art and More
by Attorney Stephen Fishman

The first book of its kind, *The Public Domain* is the definitive guide to the creative works that are not protected by copyright and can be copied freely or otherwise used without paying permission fees. Includes hundreds of resources, such as websites, libraries and archives, useful for locating public domain works.

$34.95/PUBL

CALL 800-992-6656 OR USE THE ORDER FORM IN THE BACK OF THE BOOK

CATALOG

...more from nolo.com

		PRICE	CODE

BUSINESS

	PRICE	CODE
⊙ The CA Nonprofit Corp Kit (Binder w/CD-ROM)	$39.95	CNP
▣ Consultant & Independent Contractor Agreements (Book w/Disk—PC)	$24.95	CICA
▣ The Corporate Minutes Book (Book w/Disk—PC)	$69.95	CORMI
The Employer's Legal Handbook	$31.95	EMPL
▣ Form Your Own Limited Liability Company (Book w/Disk—PC)	$34.95	LIAB
▣ Hiring Independent Contractors: The Employer's Legal Guide (Book w/Disk—PC)	$29.95	HICI
▣ How to Create a Buy-Sell Agreement and Control the Destiny of your Small Business (Book w/Disk—PC)	$49.95	BSAG
▣ How to Form a California Professional Corporation (Book w/Disk—PC)	$49.95	PROF
▣ How to Form a Nonprofit Corporation (Book w/Disk—PC)—National Edition	$39.95	NNP
How to Form a Nonprofit Corporation in California	$34.95	NON
▣ How to Form Your Own California Corporation (Binder w/Disk—PC	$39.95	CACI
▣ How to Form Your Own California Corporation (Book w/Disk—PC)	$34.95	CCOR
▣ How to Form Your Own Florida Corporation (Book w/Disk—PC)	$39.95	FLCO
▣ How to Form Your Own New York Corporation (Book w/Disk—PC)	$39.95	NYCO
▣ How to Form Your Own Texas Corporation (Book w/Disk—PC)	$39.95	TCOR
How to Write a Business Plan	$24.95	SBS
The Independent Paralegal's Handbook	$29.95	PARA
Legal Guide for Starting & Running a Small Business, Vol. 1	$24.95	RUNS
▣ Legal Guide for Starting & Running a Small Business, Vol. 2: Legal Forms (Book w/Disk—PC)	$29.95	RUNS2
Marketing Without Advertising	$19.00	MWAD
▣ Music Law (Book w/Disk—PC)	$29.95	ML
Nolo's California Quick Corp (Quick & Legal Series)	$19.95	QINC
⊙ Open Your California Business in 24 Hours (Book w/CD-ROM)	$24.95	OPEN
▣ The Partnership Book: How to Write a Partnership Agreement (Book w/Disk—PC)	$34.95	PART
Sexual Harassment on the Job	$18.95	HARS
Starting & Running a Successful Newsletter or Magazine	$24.95	MAG
Take Charge of Your Workers' Compensation Claim (California Edition)	$29.95	WORK
Tax Savvy for Small Business	$29.95	SAVVY
Trademark: Legal Care for Your Business and Product Name	$34.95	TRD

▣ Book with disk
⊙ Book with CD-ROM

CALL 800-992-6656 OR USE THE ORDER FORM IN THE BACK OF THE BOOK

	PRICE	CODE
Wage Slave No More: Law & Taxes for the Self-Employed	$24.95	WAGE
Your Rights in the Workplace	$21.95	YRW

CONSUMER

	PRICE	CODE
Fed Up with the Legal System: What's Wrong & How to Fix It	$9.95	LEG
How to Win Your Personal Injury Claim	$26.95	PICL
Nolo's Everyday Law Book	$24.95	EVL
Nolo's Pocket Guide to California Law	$12.95	CLAW
Trouble-Free Travel...And What to Do When Things Go Wrong	$14.95	TRAV

ESTATE PLANNING & PROBATE

	PRICE	CODE
8 Ways to Avoid Probate (Quick & Legal Series)	$15.95	PRO8
9 Ways to Avoid Estate Taxes (Quick & Legal Series)	$22.95	ESTX
How to Probate an Estate (California Edition)	$39.95	PAE
Make Your Own Living Trust	$24.95	LITR
Nolo's Law Form Kit: Wills	$14.95	KWL
▣ Nolo's Will Book (Book w/Disk—PC)	$29.95	SWIL
Plan Your Estate	$24.95	NEST
Quick & Legal Will Book (Quick & Legal Series)	$15.95	QUIC

FAMILY MATTERS

	PRICE	CODE
Child Custody: Building Parenting Agreements That Work	$26.95	CUST
The Complete IEP Guide	$24.95	IEP
Divorce & Money: How to Make the Best Financial Decisions During Divorce	$26.95	DIMO
Do Your Own Divorce in Oregon	$19.95	ODIV
Get a Life: You Don't Need a Million to Retire Well	$18.95	LIFE
The Guardianship Book (California Edition)	$39.95	GB
How to Adopt Your Stepchild in California	$34.95	ADOP
How to Raise or Lower Child Support in California (Quick & Legal Series)	$19.95	CHLD
A Legal Guide for Lesbian and Gay Couples	$25.95	LG
The Living Together Kit	$29.95	LTK
Nolo's Pocket Guide to Family Law	$14.95	FLD
Using Divorce Mediation: Save Your Money & Your Sanity	$21.95	UDMD

GOING TO COURT

	PRICE	CODE
Beta Your Ticket: Go To Court and Win! (National Edition)	$19.95	BEYT
Collect Your Court Judgment (California Edition)	$29.95	JUDG
The Criminal Law Handbook: Know Your Rights, Survive the System	$24.95	KYR
Everybody's Guide to Small Claims Court (National Edition)	$18.95	NSCC
Everybody's Guide to Small Claims Court in California	$18.95	CSCC
Fight Your Ticket ... and Win! (California Edition)	$19.95	FYT
How to Change Your Name in California	$34.95	NAME

▣ Book with disk

⦿ Book with CD-ROM

	PRICE	CODE
How to Mediate Your Dispute	$18.95	MEDI
How to Seal Your Juvenile & Criminal Records (California Edition)	$24.95	CRIM
How to Sue For Up to $25,000...and Win!	$29.95	MUNI
Mad at Your Lawyer	$21.95	MAD
Represent Yourself in Court: How to Prepare & Try a Winning Case	$29.95	RYC

HOMEOWNERS, LANDLORDS & TENANTS

	PRICE	CODE
▣ Contractors' and Homeowners' Guide to Mechanics' Liens (Book w/Disk—PC)	$39.95	MIEN
The Deeds Book (California Edition)	$24.95	DEED
Dog Law	$14.95	DOG
▣ Every Landlord's Legal Guide (National Edition, Book w/Disk—PC)	$34.95	ELLI
Every Tenant's Legal Guide	$26.95	EVTEN
For Sale by Owner in California	$24.95	FSBO
How to Buy a House in California	$24.95	BHCA
The Landlord's Law Book, Vol. 1: Rights & Responsibilities (California Edition)	$34.95	LBRT
The Landlord's Law Book, Vol. 2: Evictions (California Edition)	$34.95	LBEV
Leases & Rental Agreements (Quick & Legal Series)	$18.95	LEAR
Neighbor Law: Fences, Trees, Boundaries & Noise	$17.95	NEI
Renters' Rights (National Edition—Quick & Legal Series))	$15.95	RENT
Stop Foreclosure Now in California	$29.95	CLOS
Tenants' Rights (California Edition)	$21.95	CTEN

HUMOR

	PRICE	CODE
29 Reasons Not to Go to Law School	$9.95	29R
Poetic Justice	$9.95	PJ

IMMIGRATION

	PRICE	CODE
How to Get a Green Card: Legal Ways to Stay in the U.S.A.	$24.95	GRN
U.S. Immigration Made Easy	$44.95	IMEZ

MONEY MATTERS

	PRICE	CODE
▣ 101 Law Forms for Personal Use (Quick & Legal Series, Book w/disk—PC)	$24.95	SPOT
Bankruptcy: Is It the Right Solution to Your Debt Problems? (Quick & Legal Series)	$15.95	BRS
Chapter 13 Bankruptcy: Repay Your Debts	$29.95	CH13
Credit Repair (Quick & Legal Series)	$15.95	CREP
▣ The Financial Power of Attorney Workbook (Book w/disk—PC)	$24.95	FINPOA
How to File for Chapter 7 Bankruptcy	$26.95	HFB
IRAs, 401(k)s & Other Retirement Plans: Taking Your Money Out	$21.95	RET
Money Troubles: Legal Strategies to Cope With Your Debts	$19.95	MT
Nolo's Law Form Kit: Personal Bankruptcy	$16.95	KBNK
Stand Up to the IRS	$24.95	SIRS
Take Control of Your Student Loans	$19.95	SLOAN

▣ Book with disk

◉ Book with CD-ROM

PATENTS AND COPYRIGHTS

- The Copyright Handbook: How to Protect and Use Written Works (Book w/disk—PC) $29.95 — COHA
- Copyright Your Software .... $24.95 — CYS
- How to Make Patent Drawings Yourself .... $29.95 — DRAW
- The Inventor's Notebook .... $19.95 — INOT
- License Your Invention (Book w/Disk—PC) .... $39.95 — LICE
- Patent, Copyright & Trademark .... $24.95 — PCTM
- Patent It Yourself .... $46.95 — PAT
- Patent Searching Made Easy .... $24.95 — PATSE
- Software Development: A Legal Guide (Book with CD-ROM) .... $44.95 — SFT

RESEARCH & REFERENCE

- Government on the Net (Book w/CD-ROM—Windows/Macintosh) .... $39.95 — GONE
- Law on the Net (Book w/CD-ROM—Windows/Macintosh) .... $39.95 — LAWN
- Legal Research: How to Find & Understand the Law .... $24.95 — LRES
- Legal Research Made Easy (Video) .... $89.95 — LRME
- Legal Research Online & in the Library (Book w/CD-ROM—Windows/Macintosh) .... $39.95 — LRO

SENIORS

- Beat the Nursing Home Trap .... $21.95 — ELD
- The Conservatorship Book (California Edition) .... $44.95 — CNSV
- Social Security, Medicare & Pensions .... $21.95 — SOA

SOFTWARE
Call or check our website at www.nolo.com for special discounts on Software!

- LeaseWriter CD—Windows/Macintosh .... $99.95 — LWD1
- Living Trust Maker CD—Windows/Macintosh .... $79.95 — LTD2
- Small Business Legal Pro 3 CD—Windows/Macintosh .... $79.95 — SBCD3
- Personal RecordKeeper 5.0 CD—Windows/Macintosh .... $59.95 — RKD5
- Patent It Yourself CD—Windows .... $229.95 — PPC12
- WillMaker 7.0 CD—Windows/Macintosh .... $69.95 — WMD7

Special Upgrade Offer

Get 35% off the latest edition off your Nolo book

It's important to have the most current legal information. Because laws and legal procedures change often, we update our books regularly. To help keep you up-to-date we are extending this special upgrade offer. Cut out and mail the title portion of the cover of your old Nolo book and we'll give you 35% off the retail price of the NEW EDITION of that book when you purchase directly from us. For more information call us at 1-800-992-6656. This offer is to individuals only.

Order Form

Name _____

Address _____

City _____

State, Zip _____

Daytime Phone _____

E-mail _____

Our "No-Hassle" Guarantee

Return anything you buy directly from Nolo for any reason and we'll cheerfully refund your purchase price. No ifs, ands or buts.

☐ Check here if you do not wish to receive mailings from other companies

Item Code	Quantity	Item	Unit Price	Total Price

Method of payment	Subtotal
☐ Check ☐ VISA ☐ MasterCard	Add your local sales tax (California only)
☐ Discover Card ☐ American Express	Shipping: RUSH $8, Basic $3.95 (See below)
	"I bought 3, Ship it to me FREE!"(Ground shipping only)
	TOTAL

Account Number _____

Expiration Date _____

Signature _____

Shipping and Handling

Rush Delivery-Only $8

We'll ship any order to any street address in the U.S. by UPS 2nd Day Air* for only $8!

* Order by noon Pacific Time and get your order in 2 business days. Orders placed after noon Pacific Time will arrive in 3 business days. P.O. boxes and S.F. Bay Area use basic shipping. Alaska and Hawaii use 2nd Day Air or Priority Mail.

Basic Shipping—$3.95

Use for P.O. Boxes, Northern California and Ground Service.

Allow 1-2 weeks for delivery. U.S. addresses only.

For faster service, use your credit card and our toll-free numbers

Order 24 hours a day

Online	www.nolo.com
Phone	1-800-992-6656
Fax	1-800-645-0895
Mail	Nolo.com
	950 Parker St.
	Berkeley, CA 94710

Visit us online at

www.nolo.com

Take 2 minutes & Give us your 2 cents

Your comments make a big difference in the development and revision of Nolo books and software. Please take a few minutes and register your Nolo product—and your comments—with us. Not only will your input make a difference, you'll receive special offers available only to registered owners of Nolo products on our newest books and software. Register now by:

PHONE
1-800-992-6656

FAX
1-800-645-0895

EMAIL
cs@nolo.com

or **MAIL** us
this registration card

REMEMBER:
Little publishers have big ears. We really listen to you.

- fold here -

nolo REGISTRATION CARD

NAME		DATE	
ADDRESS			
CITY		STATE	ZIP
PHONE		E-MAIL	

WHERE DID YOU HEAR ABOUT THIS PRODUCT?

WHERE DID YOU PURCHASE THIS PRODUCT?

DID YOU CONSULT A LAWYER? (PLEASE CIRCLE ONE)   YES   NO   NOT APPLICABLE

DID YOU FIND THIS BOOK HELPFUL?   (VERY)   5   4   3   2   1   (NOT AT ALL)

COMMENTS

WAS IT EASY TO USE?   (VERY EASY)   5   4   3   2   1   (VERY DIFFICULT)

DO YOU OWN A COMPUTER? IF SO, WHICH FORMAT? (PLEASE CIRCLE ONE)   WINDOWS   DOS   MAC

☐ If you do not wish to receive mailings from these companies, please check this box.
☐ You can quote me in future Nolo.com promotional materials. Daytime phone number _____

DOM 1.0

NOLO IN THE NEWS

"Nolo helps lay people perform legal tasks without the aid—or fees—of lawyers."

—USA TODAY

Nolo books are ..."written in plain language, free of legal mumbo jumbo, and spiced with witty personal observations."

—ASSOCIATED PRESS

"...Nolo publications...guide people simply through the how, when, where and why of law."

—WASHINGTON POST

"Increasingly, people who are not lawyers are performing tasks usually regarded as legal work... And consumers, using books like Nolo's, do routine legal work themselves."

—NEW YORK TIMES

"...All of [Nolo's] books are easy-to-understand, are updated regularly, provide pull-out forms...and are often quite moving in their sense of compassion for the struggles of the lay reader."

—SAN FRANCISCO CHRONICLE

fold here

WITHDRAWN
No longer the property of the
Boston Public Library.
Sale of this material benefits the Library.

Place stamp here

nolo.com
950 Parker Street
Berkeley, CA 94710-9867

Attn: DOM 1.0